I0140529

A JOURNEY OF RICHES

Unlock Your Hidden Potential

13 Stories to Transform obstacles into infinite possibilities

A Journey of Riches: Unlock Your Hidden Potential
13 Stories to Transform obstacles into infinite possibilities

Published by Motion Media International
Editors: Eric Wyman, Yasmin Phillip, Parker Hansen, Rosemary Lawton, Arynne Priest, and Pamela Minch
Cover Design: Motion Media International
Typesetting & Assembly: Motion Media International

Printing: Amazon and Ingram Sparks
Creator: John Spender - Primary Author
Title: *A Journey of Riches: Unlock Your Hidden Potential*

ISBN Digital: 978-1-925919-85-1
ISBN Print: 978-1-925919-86-8
Subjects: Motivation, Inspiration, Memoir

ACKNOWLEDGMENTS

Reading and writing are gifts that very few give to themselves. It is such a powerful way to reflect and gain closure from the past; reading and writing are therapeutic processes. The experience raises one's self-esteem, confidence, and awareness of self.

I learned this when I collated the first book in the *A Journey of Riches* series, which now includes 39 books with over 350 co-authors from over 50 countries. Writing about your personal experiences is difficult, and I honor and respect every author who has collaborated in the series.

For many authors, English is their second language, which is a significant achievement. In creating this anthology of short stories, I have been touched by the generosity, gratitude, and shared energy this experience has given everyone.

The inspiration for *A Journey of Riches - Unlock your Hidden Potential* was born from my desire to share empowering stories to unleash your full capabilities. Each chapter is written by a different author sharing their wisdom on the power of continuous growth to live life to the fullest.

I want to thank all the authors for entrusting me with their unique memories, encounters, and wisdom. Thank you for sharing and opening the door to your soul so others may learn from your experience. I trust the readers will gain confidence from your successes and wisdom from your failures.

I also want to thank my family. I know you are proud of me, seeing how far I have come from that ten-year-old boy learning to read and write at a basic level. So big shout out to Mom, Robert, Dad, and Merril; my brother Adam and his daughter Krystal; my sister Hollie and her partner Brian; my nephew Charlie and niece, Heidi; thank you for your support. Also, kudos to my grandparents, Gran and Pop, who are alive and well, and Ma and Pa, who now rest in peace. They accept me just as I am with all my travels and adventures worldwide.

Thanks to the team at Motion Media International; you have done an excellent job editing and collating this book. It was a pleasure working with you on this successful project, and I thank you for your patience in dealing with the changes and adjustments along the way.

Thank you, the reader, for having the courage to examine your life and consider how you can improve your future in a rapidly changing world.

Again, thank you to my co-authors: **Grandmother Mulara, Ewelina Korus, Darlene Doiron, Rebecca Shannon, Catalina Galeano, Laura Jean Denman, Corrina Bowcott, Lynn Hayward, Patrick Richard Garcia, Cari Rickabaugh, Ben Welch and Annelise Pesa.**

With gratitude,
John Spender

TABLE OF CONTENTS

Praise for *A Journey of Riches Book Series*

"The *A Journey of Riches* book series is a great collection of inspiring short stories that will leave you wanting more!"
~ Alex Hoffmann, Network Marketing Guru

"If you are looking for an inspiring read to get you through any change, this is it! This book comprises many gripping perspectives from a collection of successful international authors with a tone of wisdom to share."
~ Theera Phetmalaigul, Entrepreneur/Investor

"*A Journey of Riches* is an empowering series that implements two simple words for overcoming life's struggles.

By diving into the meaning of the words 'problem' and 'challenge,' you will be motivated to believe in the triumph of perseverance. With many different authors from all around the world coming together to share various stories of life's trials, you will find yourself drenched in encouragement to push through even the darkest of battles. The stories are heartfelt personal shares of moving through and transforming challenges into rich life experiences.

The book will move, touch, and inspire your spirit to face and overcome life's adversities. It is a truly inspirational read. Thank you for being the kind, open soul you are, John!"
~ Casey Plouffe, Seven Figure Network Marketer

"A must-read for anyone facing major changes or challenges in life right now. This book will give you the courage to overcome any struggle with confidence, grace, and ease."
~ Jo-Anne Irwin, Transformational Coach and Best-Selling Author

"I have enjoyed the *A Journey of Riches* book series. Each person's story is written from the heart, and everyone's journey is different. However, we all have a story to tell, and John Spender does an amazing job of finding authors and combining their stories into uplifting books."
~ Liz Misner Palmer, Foreign Service Officer

"A timely read as I'm facing a few challenges right now. I like the various insights from the different authors. This book will inspire you to move through any challenge or change you are experiencing."
~ David Ostrand, Business Owner

"I've known John Spender for a while now, and I was blessed with an opportunity to be in book four in the series. I know that you will enjoy this new journey, like the rest of the books in the series. The collection of stories will assist you with making changes, dealing with challenges, and seeing that transformation is possible for your life."
~ Charlie O'Shea, Entrepreneur

"*A Journey of Riches* series will draw you in and help you dig deep into your soul. These authors have unbelievable life stories of purpose inside of them. John Spender is dedicated to bringing peace, love, and adventure to the world of his readers! Dive into this series, and you will be transformed!"
~ Jeana Matichak, Author of *Finding Peace*

"Awesome! Truly inspirational! It is amazing what the human spirit can achieve and overcome! Highly recommended!"
~ Fabrice Beliard, Australian Business Coach and Best-Selling Author

"*A Journey of Riches* series is a must-read. It is an empowering collection of inspirational and moving stories full of courage, strength, and heart. Bringing peace and awareness to those lucky enough to read to assist and inspire them on their life journey."
~ Gemma Castiglia, Avalon Healing, Best-Selling Author

"The *A Journey of Riches* book series is an inspirational collection of books that will empower you to take on any challenge or change in life."
~ Kay Newton, Midlife Stress Buster, and Best-Selling Author

"*A Journey of Riches* book series is an inspiring collection of stories, sharing many different ideas and perspectives on how to overcome challenges, deal with change, and make empowering choices in your life. Open the book anywhere and let your mood choose where you need to read. Buy one of the books today; you'll be glad that you did!"
~ Trish Rock, Modern Day Intuitive, Best-Selling Author, Speaker, Psychic & Holistic Coach

"*A Journey of Riches* is another inspiring read. The authors are from all over the world, and each has a unique perspective to share that will have you thinking differently about your current circumstances in life. An insightful read!"
~ Alexandria Calamel, Success Coach and Best-Selling Author

"The *A Journey of Riches* book series is a collection of real-life stories, which are truly inspiring and give you the confidence that no matter what you are dealing with in your life, there is a light at the end of the tunnel and a very bright one at that. Totally empowering!"
~ John Abbott, Freedom Entrepreneur

"An amazing collection of true stories from individuals who have overcome great changes and who have transformed their lives and used their experience to uplift, inspire, and support others."
~ Carol Williams, Author, Speaker & Coach

"You can empower yourself from the power within this book that can help awaken the sleeping giant within you. John has a purpose in life to bring inspiring people together to share their wisdom for the benefit of all who venture deep into this book series. If you are looking for inspiration to be someone special, this book can be your guide."
~ Bill Bilwani, Renowned Melbourne Restaurateur

"In the *A Journey of Riches* series, you will catch the impulse to step up, reconsider, and settle for only the very best for yourself and those around you. Penned from the heart and with an unflinching drive to make a difference for the good of all, *A Journey of Riches* series is a must-read."
~ Steve Coleman, author of *Decisions, Decisions! How to Make the Right One Every Time*

"Do you want to be on top of your game? *A Journey of Riches* is a must-read with breakthrough insights that will help you do just that!"
~ Christopher Chen, Entrepreneur

"In *A Journey of Riches*, you will find the insight, resources, and tools you need to transform your life. By reading the author's stories, you, too, can be inspired to achieve your greatest accomplishments and what is truly possible for you. Reading this book activates your true potential for transforming your life way beyond what you think is possible. Read it and learn how you, too, can have a magical life."
~ Elaine Mc Guinness, Best-Selling Author of *Unleash Your Authentic Self!*

"If you are looking for an inspiring read, look no further than the *A Journey of Riches* book series. The books are an inspiring collection of short stories that will encourage you to embrace life even more. I highly recommend you read one of the books today!"
~ Kara Dono, Doula, Healer, and Best-Selling Author

"The *A Journey of Riches* book series is filled with real-life short stories of heartfelt tribulations turned into uplifting self-transformation by the power of the human spirit to overcome adversity. The journeys captured in these books will encourage you to embrace life in a whole new way. I highly recommend reading this inspiring anthology series."
~ Chris Drabenstott, Best-Selling Author and Editor

"There is so much motivational power in the *A Journey of Riches* series!! Each book is a compilation of inspiring, real-life stories by several different authors, which makes the journey feel more relatable and success more attainable. If you are looking for something to move you forward, you'll find it in one (or all) of these books."
~ Cary MacArthur, Personal Empowerment Coach

"I've been fortunate to write with John Spender, and now, I call him a friend. *A Journey of Riches* book series features real stories that have inspired me and will inspire you. John has a passion for finding amazing people from all over the world, giving the series a global perspective on relevant subject matters."
~ Mike Campbell, Fat Guy Diary, LLC

"The *A Journey of Riches* series is the reflection of beautiful souls who have discovered the fire within. Each story takes you inside the truth of what truly matters in life. While reading these stories, my heart space expanded to understand that our most significant contribution in this lifetime is to give and receive love. May you also feel inspired as you read this book."
~ Katie Neubaum, Author of *Transformation Calling*

"*A Journey of Riches* is an inspiring testament that love and gratitude are the secret ingredients to living a happy and fulfilling life. This series is sure to inspire and bless your life in a big way. Truly an inspirational read that is written and created by real people, sharing real-life stories about the power and courage of the human spirit."
~ Jen Valadez, Emotional Intuitive and Best-Selling Author

"If you are looking for an inspirational read, look no further than the *A Journey of Riches* book series. The books are an inspiring and educational collection of short stories from the author's soul that will encourage you to embrace life even more. I've even given them to my clients, too, so that their journeys inspire them in life for wealth, health, and everything else in between. I recommend you make it a priority to read one of the books today!"
~ Goro Gupta, Chief Education Officer, Mortgage Terminator, Property Mentor

PREFACE

I collated this book and chose authors from around the world to share their experiences about what "Unlock Your Hidden Potential" meant to them. This book is the collective wisdom of the various authors' journeys to unleash their inner strength. This eclectic collection of chapters encompasses many different writing styles and perspectives that embrace the intelligence of our hearts and intuition.

Like all of us, each author has a unique story and insight to share with you. One or more authors might have lived through an experience like one in your life. Their words could be just what you need to read to help you through your challenges and inspire you to continue your chosen path.

Storytelling is how humankind communicates ideas and learns throughout our civilization. While we have become more sophisticated with technology, and life in the modern world is now more convenient, there is still much discontent and dissatisfaction. Many people have also moved away from reading books and are missing valuable information that can help them move forward with a positive outlook. Moving toward the tasks or dreams that scare us breeds confidence in growing towards becoming better versions of ourselves.

I think it is essential to turn off the television, slow down, read, reflect, and take the time to appreciate everything you have in life. Start with an anthology book as they offer a cornucopia of viewpoints relating to a particular theme. Here, it's unlocking hidden potential and how others have tapped into theirs. We feel stuck in life or have challenges in a particular area because we see the problem through the same lens that created it. With this compendium and all the books in the *A Journey of Riches* series, you have many writing styles and perspectives that will help you think and see your challenges differently, motivating you to elevate your circumstances.

Anthology books are also great because you can start from any chapter and gain valuable insight or a nugget of wisdom without the feeling that you have missed something from the earlier episodes.

I love reading many personal development books because learning and personal growth is vital. If you are not learning and growing, you're staying the same. Everything in the universe is growing, expanding, and changing. If we are not open to different ideas and ways of thinking and being, then even the most skilled and educated can become close-minded.

This book series aims to open you up to diverse ways of perceiving your reality. It encourages and gives you many avenues of thinking about the same subject. I wish for you to feel empowered to make a decision that will best suit you in moving forward with your life. As Albert Einstein said, "We **cannot solve problems with the same level of thinking that created them."** So, with Einstein's words in mind, let your mood pick a chapter, or read from the beginning to the end, and be guided to find the answers you seek.

With gratitude,
John Spender

"Unlock your potential by believing that the impossible is possible."

~ Jim Rohn

CHAPTER ONE

The Warrior's Journey: The Path to Self-Discovery

By Catalina Galeano

This chapter is dedicated to my daughter and mentor, Isabella Valentina Moreno.

There comes a pivotal moment in life when everything you thought you were—the identity shaped by expectations, past experiences, and societal conditioning—must shatter. No matter how much you've achieved or how far you've come, a deep-seated emptiness may linger within you, growing louder whenever you drift away from your inner truth. This chapter extends a heartfelt invitation to embark on a profound journey of self-discovery, urging you to uncover the essence of who you truly are, unbound by the stories, roles, and layers that have defined you until now.

Connecting with your authenticity is the most profound act of self-love. This connection reveals the keys to unlocking your highest potential and aligning your life with your deepest values, purpose, and divine mission. True transformation begins when we peel back the layers of conditioning and rediscover the parts of ourselves that have always been whole, powerful, and true. This journey encourages you to explore your divine nature, shedding the false identity constructed by ego, culture, and society while reclaiming the essence that resides within your very DNA—the ancient wisdom and unique gifts that define your soul.

Only through this breaking, this shedding of what no longer serves you, can your real and boundless potential emerge. When the layers fall away, you catch a glimpse of the limitless truth of who you are. In these moments, your essence becomes clear, not simply as a reflection of your life but as the very force that gives life its deepest meaning.

This is a process of rebirth, an opportunity to let go of the identities that no longer fit, enabling you to create a life that resonates with your truest self and highest aspirations.

In a world that often measures worth by achievements and external success, we are taught to seek approval and validation by meeting the expectations of others, gradually losing sight of what sets our souls on fire. Yet, true transformation is only possible when we look within—when we question the structures we've accepted as "normal" and begin to break down the limitations we've unknowingly placed on ourselves.

From a very young age, I've sensed the power of this truth. I have always been the one who dared to question, to feel deeply, and to live passionately and authentically. My path wasn't about fitting into a mold; it was about breaking free from it. This journey, unconventional as it might seem, was the only one that could lead me to the freedom and clarity I hold today.

I realized that the greatest risk wasn't in walking an unknown path but in abandoning the calling of my own soul.

The truth is that if you want to unlock your highest potential, you must first recognize who you are not. This unraveling requires courage because it means facing the parts of yourself shaped by others' expectations, those parts built around fear and ego that have separated you from the divine essence of your being. But each challenge, every pain, every doubt is an invitation to peel back these layers and step closer to your true self.

In releasing these layers, you'll see that discomfort and struggle are not punishments but catalysts—agents of transformation and growth. Every hardship is a chance to reshape your reality and reclaim your innate power. It is within the discomfort that you find your strength, and within the breaking that you remember what has always been whole.

To transform, you must be willing to step into the unknown and embrace the vulnerability of change. Only then can you open the doorway to your highest potential. This process of un-becoming—of dismantling the old to make space for the new—is where we truly embody the magnificence of who we are.

Your life holds this same potential. Whatever emptiness you feel is not there to defeat you; it is there to guide you back to the truth of your soul. In these pages, I invite you to uncover your authentic self—the version of you that is unbound by fear or limitation, the version that has always existed beneath the surface, waiting to be set free.

This journey is not for the faint-hearted; it's for those ready to awaken to their fullest power. It's for those willing to rise above conformity and embrace the life they were truly meant to live. This is your invitation to transform, evolve, and step into the most powerful expression of yourself.

The Power of Self-Inquiry: Discovering Your Divine Essence

Have you ever paused amidst the noise of life and asked yourself: **Who am I?** This simple yet profound question holds the key to unlocking the deepest layers of your being. It's not about your name, your career, or your accomplishments but about something far greater—your true, divine essence. This essence is the source of your strength, your clarity, and your potential to transcend any challenge life presents. The journey to self-discovery is not just an exploration of your identity but a path toward unlocking the limitless potential of your natural gifts.

The Depth of the Question: Who Am I?

When asked who we are, most of us instinctively respond with what we do or what we have: “I’m a doctor,” “I graduated from X university,” or “I work in Y industry.” These roles and titles, while part of our lives, do not define the essence of who we are. They are external identities, and although they may bring a sense of security or achievement, they remain transient and superficial.

The truth of who you are transcends all of these labels. **You are not your profession, your possessions, your relationships, or even the experiences you’ve accumulated.** The journey of self-inquiry begins by shedding these identities and diving into the infinite, untouched part of you that exists beyond them. This is where your divine essence resides—an essence that is eternal, infinite, and interconnected with the fabric of life itself.

The Power of Knowing What You Are Not

To uncover who you truly are, you must first explore what you are **not**. Take a moment to reflect and list all the ways you have identified yourself over the years: your job title, your role in relationships, your societal status, even the car you drive or the clothes you wear. Now, ask yourself: **Are these things really me?** Do they capture the vastness of my spirit?

When you begin to strip away these false identifiers, you are left with a space—a space that may feel unfamiliar at first but is rich with potential. It's like peeling back layers of an onion until you reach the core, where your true essence lies. This practice is often called "neti neti" in ancient wisdom traditions, which means "not this, not that," and invites you to reject each false identity until you arrive at the essence of your being.

And what is that essence? It is the pure **I Am**—the powerful statement of existence that defines your true reality. What follows the words "I AM" shapes your world. If you fill that space with limiting labels, you confine yourself to them. But when you fill it with words of empowerment, love, and truth, you align with the highest version of yourself.

The Divine Essence of I AM

"I Am" is not just a phrase; it is the most powerful declaration in the universe. It connects you to your soul's potential, to the vastness of your being, and to the divine energy that flows through all creation. What follows "I Am" is not merely descriptive—it is **creative**. The words you attach to this phrase become the blueprint of your reality. This is why it is so vital to choose your words and thoughts with care.

Imagine saying, "I am love. I am kind. I am infinite potential." When you embrace these truths, you begin to embody them. You start to live from a place of deep connection to your essence rather than from the expectations or limitations imposed upon you by the external world. You realize that you are the breath in your lungs, the clarity of your mind, and the love in your heart. You are a channel for divine wisdom, an expression of infinite creativity, and a vessel for unconditional love.

From this place, you recognize that you are not bound by your circumstances or the labels society has given you. Instead, you are aligned with the power of creation itself, capable of manifesting your highest potential.

Unleashing Your Natural Gifts from this Space

Once you connect with your divine essence, the natural gifts within you begin to emerge effortlessly. These gifts are not something you need to chase or earn—they are already present within you, waiting to be remembered and expressed. When you operate from a place of deep self-awareness, these gifts flow naturally because they are an extension of your true self.

What are these gifts? They vary from person to person. For some, it may be the gift of healing or intuition. For others, it could be music, art, communication, teaching, creativity, leadership, resilience, or problem-solving. Whatever your natural gifts are, they are uniquely yours, and they are most powerfully expressed when you are grounded in your essence.

The more you practice self-inquiry, the more you will uncover the vastness of your inner resources. You will find that you have access to an incredible wellspring of potential—one that goes far beyond the limitations of the mind or ego. This is the place where your greatest contributions to the world will emerge, not from a place of striving but from a place of **Being**.

A Journey Back to Yourself

Engaging in self-inquiry is an invitation to come home to yourself. It is a practice of remembering that beneath all the layers of external identities and roles, you are pure consciousness, love, and divine energy. And from that place, you have the power to create, heal, and transform not only your life but the lives of those around you.

So, I invite you to sit with this question: **Who am I?** Don't rush to find an answer. Allow the question to sit with you in silence, in meditation. Let it unfold naturally as the layers of illusion dissolve, revealing the brilliance of your divine essence.

As you discover who you truly are, you will not only gain profound insight into yourself but will also tap into the boundless potential of your natural gifts. You are here not just to exist but to **thrive**, to express the fullness of your being and to shine your light brightly in the world.

The Dismantling Process: Connecting with Your Core Values

Have you ever truly reflected on what fuels your soul and what values form the foundation of your existence? These values are far more than temporary ideas or abstract principles; they are the unwavering lights that guide you toward your highest purpose. They are the standards you hold, the non-negotiables that you will stand by, no matter the circumstances or challenges that life presents.

Core values act as your internal compass, helping to shape the decisions and actions that lead you closer to your true self. When you're deeply connected with what matters most, decision-making becomes clearer, more aligned with your soul's path, and infused with a sense of purpose. This alignment is where true fulfillment arises—not from external achievements or recognition, but from living authentically and intentionally.

By identifying and connecting with your core values, you tap into the key that unlocks your highest potential. It's not just about creating a life that appears successful by society's standards; it's about crafting a life that is deeply meaningful and true to who you are at your essence. When you live in alignment with these values, you not only achieve personal fulfillment but also experience the profound satisfaction of living in harmony with your authentic self.

This is the gateway to a life rich in purpose and true to your soul's deepest callings.

After years of self-discovery, navigating life's trials, and engaging in deep healing modalities—including the transformative power of plant medicine—I uncovered the values that breathe life into my being. I found that my purpose revolved around being of service, adding value to others' lives, and speaking my truth, no matter the discomfort. Being in integrity with myself and my mission became non-negotiable.

When I learned to speak from my heart, and aligned my actions with my values, I discovered something powerful: life began to unfold in ways I hadn't anticipated. Opportunities appeared, people who resonated with my energy were drawn into my life, and doors I never expected to open began to swing wide. This is the undeniable power of living in alignment with your essence. It's not just about doing more or working harder; it's about *being* more of who you are. From that place, the right connections and opportunities naturally follow.

Your essence is your medicine. When you live in congruence with your values, people can feel it. You create an energetic ripple effect, impacting the lives of those around you, not just by what you do but by the authenticity and care with which you do it.

Now it's your turn to uncover the values that will shape your path to your highest potential. Take a moment to grab a piece of paper, sit with yourself, and ask:

1. *What moves my soul?*

2. *What passions make me feel alive?*

3. *What values guide my decisions and actions?*

4. *What are the non-negotiables in my life?*

As you write down these answers, don't stop at vague ideas. Push deeper. How do these values appear in your relationships, career, and everyday life? What kind of person do you want to become by living in alignment with these principles? What values will hold you accountable as you evolve, and how can you fully embody them?

Radical honesty is crucial here. The more truthful you are with yourself, the closer you move toward vibrating in a frequency that is fully aligned with your fullest potential. When you embody your values with unwavering authenticity, you begin to attract people, circumstances, and opportunities that are in harmony with the life you are here to create.

Remember, living in alignment with your values isn't just a philosophy, it's a practice! The more you ground yourself in what truly matters to you, the more magnetic your life becomes. You will find that life doesn't need to be forced; it flows naturally when you are in tune with your core. This is where your transformation begins. This is where your highest potential awakens.

Noble Silence: The Gateway to Your Divine Essence

In the modern world, noise often fills the spaces where silence could offer us the most profound transformation. Yet, in silence, we encounter the most potent tool for self-discovery: the stillness of our own being. I learned this deeply in 2008 when I embarked on a ten-day silent meditation retreat that dismantled the very identity I had clung to for years. It was within those quiet, uncomfortable moments that I unearthed the gift of true self-awareness. Through the discomfort, my inner wisdom surfaced—guiding me away from the ego's grip and toward a new clarity I had never experienced before.

In silence, something extraordinary happens: the voice of the ego, always demanding attention, begins to quiet. By day four of the retreat, the incessant inner dialogue—the noise of fear, self-judgment, and attachment to who I *thought* I was—began to dissolve. I felt the ego resisting, fighting for control, because it knew what was coming. On day five, the noise ceased entirely. What replaced it was an unshakeable peace, a sense of profound stillness that opened the doorway to my essence. I discovered that in the absence of noise, I was not *"doing"* anything to be valuable. I was simply *being*, and in that being, I accessed a profound connection to my divine potential.

When we let go of the identity constructed by external forces—society, culture, even our own limiting beliefs—what we find is the purest version of ourselves. Toltec wisdom tells us that "self-importance" is the source of suffering. When we are constantly worried about how others perceive us, we give away our power. But in silence, we don't need to perform, prove, or defend who we are. We simply witness the truth that is already within.

Let me ask you: How often do you give yourself the gift of silence? How long do you allow yourself to sit with nothing but your breath, your heartbeat, your presence? This practice, though simple, is extremely challenging yet profoundly transformative. When you sit in silence, you detach from the noise of the external world, from the constant pull of the ego, and you connect with your true essence. It's in this space that your natural gifts, the ones that have always been a part of you, begin to reveal themselves.

By day seven of my retreat, I began to experience heightened clarity, even clairvoyant abilities. I could anticipate events with precision. I didn't need to speak of them or seek validation. The experience itself was the lesson. The longer I remained in silence, the more I realized that by shedding my old identity—by letting go of the need to control how others saw me—I was opening myself to receive a deeper wisdom, a divine knowing that is always present, waiting for us to listen.

The beauty of silence is that it is both a refuge and a guide. It leads us away from the incessant chatter of the mind and into a space of profound clarity. When you engage in a daily practice of silence and meditation—even for just fifteen minutes—you begin to shift. Your mind rewires itself, no longer gripped by fear, ego, or attachment to outcomes. You become attuned to a greater intelligence, one that doesn't rely on external validation but is grounded in inner truth and universal wisdom.

Take a moment right now to connect with your breath. Let go of everything you think you are—your name, your roles, your expectations. Drop into the stillness of your heart and expand that energy throughout your entire body. Observe how your body responds—how your shoulders relax, your breath deepens, and a profound tranquility washes over you.

This is the space where transformation begins. From this place of silence, your divine potential will naturally emerge.

Remember this: Silence and meditation are not just tools for relaxation. They are the keys to unlocking your greatest gifts. These practices guide you to the essence of who you truly are, stripping away the layers of conditioning and identity that have kept you small. In the quiet of your being, you will find the holy grail of your deepest potential, waiting to be unleashed.

So, I invite you to sit in silence, to let go of the old stories, and to allow the wisdom of your own essence to guide you forward. It is within this silence that the true magic of life begins to unfold and where your highest potential comes to life.

Embracing Uncertainty to Find Your True Calling

When you reach a profound clarity about who you are—when you align with your deepest truth, peel away the layers of old structures, and fully connect with your natural gifts, the universe takes notice. Life will challenge you, pushing you to step forward and prove that you are ready to act boldly on a path toward true fulfillment. It is in these moments, standing at the edge of the familiar and the unknown, that your commitment is tested. Are you prepared to embrace the journey that will awaken the highest version of yourself?

In 2021, I entered a transformative journey that redefined my life through surrender, resilience, and an unshakeable connection to my heart's deepest calling. During an Ayahuasca ceremony, Divine Grandmother spoke directly to my soul: "If you don't fully embody your natural gifts and reclaim the mission of your heart, your body will begin to wither." Her message was clear and urgent. I was living a life disconnected from purpose, caught in the corporate grind where I worked with high-level executives across industries, managing operations, finances, and investor relations. Despite the steady income and societal recognition, something essential was missing. I felt drained, uninspired, and profoundly out of touch with my truth. My life had become a cycle of enabling others' dreams while my own faded. My body mirrored this inner emptiness. My hair began falling out and numbness settled over me, leaving me without a sense of direction or vitality.

After that ceremony and the clear message from the divine spirit, I couldn't unhear the calling. I knew I had to leave the job that was draining my spirit and finally pursue my heart's true mission—to become a certified coach. For as long as I can remember, I have been passionate about studying the complexities of the human mind, exploring psychology, and understanding human behavior. I deeply enjoyed creating meaningful connections and safe spaces where vulnerable conversations could emerge, allowing true healing to take place.

It felt audacious, even terrifying, to leave stability behind. But I remembered how, throughout my life, people had been inexplicably drawn to me, sharing their innermost thoughts in my presence and finding comfort and clarity. My gift had always been this ability to hold sacred space, allowing others to release, to express without fear or judgment, and to uncover answers already alive within them. Friends and strangers alike often said, "Cata, you were born to help people. You create a space where healing happens naturally." Yet, it had never dawned on me that I could turn this calling into my life's work. That all changed the day I finally listened to my heart's voice and committed to my certification. For six months, I lived on my savings, fueled by a single, unwavering truth: I was finally pursuing my mission.

It wasn't easy. As the sole provider for my daughter, I faced moments of fear and doubt, wondering if I'd made a mistake. But in those times of uncertainty, I anchored myself in my purpose, trusting in the undeniable knowing that I was building a life aligned with my soul. Walking through fear and embracing uncertainty taught me that resilience isn't just a quality—it's a pathway to transformation. Only by daring to leave the familiar can we dismantle old programming and rebuild our minds to recognize our true potential. The mindset we cultivate in these moments defines everything. When we step beyond our comfort zones, we unlock a level of greatness we never knew existed.

This journey wasn't just about changing careers; it was about awakening my soul's essence and reclaiming my truth. Through every challenge, I stayed radically honest with myself, committed to living in alignment with my values and the mission that lights me up from within. This path has brought me home to my authentic self, showing me that our highest potential lies on the other side of fear, waiting for us to step boldly toward it.

Today, I happily lead a successful coaching practice, catalyzing profound transformation. I help individuals reconnect with their natural essence and authentic truth, empowering them to create a life with purpose, passion, and fulfillment.

Now, think of the journey you're being called to as a conversation with your soul, one that invites you to come closer to what truly matters. Take this time to *actively reconnect* with your inner voice. Start with a simple, powerful practice: each day, write down one small step you can take to honor the longing within you. These steps don't have to be monumental, just something that feels *true* to you.

Ask yourself:

1. *What would I pursue if I knew I couldn't fail?*
2. *What would I create if I knew my only purpose was to feel deeply alive?*
3. *How would it feel to live each day in alignment with my soul's purpose and natural abilities?*
4. *How would my relationships, work, and self-worth evolve if I honored my deepest gifts and authentic desires?*

Allow yourself to explore these questions without judgment. Maybe it's a conversation you've been avoiding, a new path you've been hesitant to follow, or an old pattern you're ready to release.

This is your invitation to step onto a path of deeper authenticity and self-discovery. Begin by practicing radical honesty with yourself. Name the fears that have held you back, acknowledge the dreams that won't let go, and commit to honoring them. And each time doubt arises, return to the truth of your purpose, to the fire that inspires your heart, trusting that every small action adds up to unchaining your potential.

As you make these daily choices, watch how your life begins to shift, how doors you didn't even see start to open. **This is how your highest potential reveals itself—not in the absence of fear but in the courage to listen, to act, and to believe in the power of your journey.**

I want you to remember this: true success is not defined by how many people know your name **but by how deeply you know yourself.** Real success lies in understanding the unique gifts you possess and how they can serve the greater good. When we awaken to the profound truth that the power and essence we have been seeking have always resided within us, we step into our roles as both architects and alchemists of our own destinies.

This is your call to action: embark on a journey of self-discovery that honors every joy, every sorrow, and every lesson that life offers. Begin to see your existence through the eyes of the divine and recognize that you are here to create a masterpiece—your life. Embrace every process, for it is through this journey that your highest potential unfolds. You are the artist, the creator, and the creation. Now is the moment to rise and unleash the most beautiful expression of your true self. Your story is waiting to be written, so make it a masterpiece!

"Unless you do something beyond what you have done, you will never grow or experience your full potential."
—Unknown

"The only way to discover the limits of the possible is to go beyond them into the impossible."

~ Arthur C. Clarke

CHAPTER TWO

I Believe in Pink

By Rebecca Shannon

We express ourselves in countless ways—through our work, our creations, and how we show up in the world. For me, that vibrant expression bursts forth in hot pink, a color that embodies passion, playfulness, and limitless potential. It radiates joy and a love for life, weaving a bright thread through the tapestry of my existence. As I sit here, reflecting on the profound impact of this color, I can see it as clearly as the stars shimmering in the night sky.

Embracing pink is not just about the color for me; it's about authenticity and becoming the fullest version of myself. The energy of hot pink envelops me. It's in my home, my branding, my writing, and—without a doubt—in my wardrobe. The ripples I create through this color sparkle and shine, attracting incredible opportunities and relationships into my life. This hot pink thread has not only unlocked my potential but has connected me to extraordinary people, experiences, and a world I've come to love deeply. Let me explain…

One of our greatest gifts is the ability to be fully expressed and seen. By weaving hot pink into my identity, I've discovered a powerful way to serve others. In my coaching, speaking, and writing, this vibrant energy flows through everything I do, creating a magnetic pull that encourages others to embrace their colors, to paint their lives with whatever colors ignite their passions.

The hot pink ripples I create sparkle and shine all over the world. I am the energetic match for this passionate color. Pink has allowed me to become the fully expressed version of myself. What people see when they are drawn to the hot pink coat is its clash with bright orange in the latest branding shots. What they feel is a resonance in color, in how I sparkle and shine—they see the love, the passion and the purpose. It makes them smile, and they are lifted, inspired and energized.

Our Deepest Fear by Marianne Williamson is a piece of writing that has shown up so often in my life, and the words "as we let our own light shine, we unconsciously give other people permission to do the same" is a guiding principle for the work I do. I now consciously choose to shine that light so others can do the same, including you! It's a less unconscious action now, and as I write, the transformative power of this simple color choice still amazes me. This hot pink thread has led to an extraordinary life of purpose, connection, and fulfillment I could only have dreamed of a few years ago. The significance of pink in my personal and professional life is such a powerful reminder of my passion, intuition, and determination.

Have you ever experienced a moment that changed the course of your life? The truth is that every moment does. In every moment, we get to unlock a little more of our potential. In every moment, we get to create a new possibility. If we look back, there are moments that stand out as the ones that changed everything. They shine a little brighter in the constellation of the lives we have lived, sometimes lived well and sometimes lived through. Each moment is a guiding light when we look back and see how we were always unlocking and creating the lives we live today.

My words are inspired by the famous Steve Jobs commencement speech at Stanford in 2005. In the speech, Steve speaks of how he connected the 'dots' in his past, moments that led him to create so much in cutting-edge technology, influential in unlocking potential of so many other people either directly through the technology he created, inspired by his story or called forward by the phenomenon that is the iconic Apple brand.

I see those dots as stars. "You can't connect the stars by looking forward; you can only connect them looking backward. You must trust that the stars will somehow connect in your future. Trust in something, trust intuition, trust life, trust the signs and synchronicities. You get to connect the stars to align and support your dreams. Believe in yourself. Trust in your leadership. Trust in the unique constellations you create."

For it is in trust that we unlock our hidden potential. If unlimited potential were a cake, trust would be the eggs, action would be the flour and reflection would be the pink icing on top!

So, this is me connecting the stars in hindsight and sharing my constellation with you. Just like the recent Northern lights, the Aurora Borealis, that lit up the sky this month over my Creekside home in Kent in the UK—they were pink.

The hot pink that shines bright in the world was created in those moments, those stars that were to light up so much for my future. I would never have connected those by looking forward, but looking back, they create the most incredible journey. I can see the stars were always shining, and I was intuitively following my passion and purpose, always trusting that I would create an extraordinary world filled with possibility.

If you'd asked me in the past, I would have said that pink was never my color, and yet I have found the cutest pictures of me as a sugar plum fairy in an early ballet show, maybe six or seven years old. My hair was tied up in little buns with a pink ribbon, my sweet ballet dress was edged in pink, and even—I imagine much to my mother's horror—a bright pink lipstick was smeared on my lips with pink blush on my cheeks, just above my dimples. Have you ever met a true angel that doesn't have dimples? Embracing my inner angel has allowed me to believe in my potential and to step out of my comfort zone again and again.

Fast forward a few years, and under another star, there is a picture of me in my twenties, reclining on a yacht in the Caribbean, wearing denim cutoff jeans and an itsy bitsy pink bikini! A few more years and fabulous at forty, there I am in Saint Lucia under a waterfall, arms outstretched in a hot pink two-piece. These are all the moments that I can see looking back, glimmers of the pink angel I was to become. My past self had created stars that would light the path to my future.

On an ordinary day shopping in London, a vibrant pink wool coat stood out from all the muted winter colors on a rail right next to the counter as I was paying. That was the moment that began to draw all these perfect pink stars together and unlock a future that I had not yet realized was possible. I picked out the coat and added it to the other pieces on the counter. The young woman looked up as she scanned the ticket. "I love pink. This will look fabulous on you," she said. I smiled as she handed me the bag and I headed out of the store. What we choose to wear directly affects how we feel, and feelings are the key to embracing our fullest potential.

The coat became a favorite that winter. I was in the process of separating from my husband and there were difficult conversations to be had in a cold, colorless room in our local community center. Discussions mediated by a stranger about a life I did not see myself in. Finances were divided up on whiteboards with totals in pounds earned, saved or spent. There were no columns for love, support, loss, grief or motherhood. The boards were white, the words and numbers in black. The only colour a red underlining or circling bits that the other stranger in the room and I could not agree on. It reminded me of homework returned with all the corrections in red pen, all the things I had gotten wrong for everyone to see. I felt completely out of my depth. Powerless and fighting a battle I had never wanted; a battle I knew I wouldn't win. I felt drained, exhausted and empty. I couldn't find myself; I had become lost in this life. I felt as colourless as the cold room we were in.

I purposefully wore the coat to give me confidence. It was a heavy wool mix, long and elegant—it felt like a majestic robe, allowing me to embody the Queen energy I needed to hold myself together for those awful meetings that stripped me bare of my value, leaving me full of shame for all I had not been and everything I believed I had broken and could not fix. Underneath the black jeans and jumper I wore—hidden for only me to know—were hot pink matching undies that provided a whole other level of energy.

A few months later, I arrived for a week intensive as part of my coaching training with the women's empowerment community One of Many. Their brilliant marketing slogans "Are you Superwoman? Do you feel like you are barely surviving? Are your relationships falling apart around you?" caught my attention in the aftermath of the marriage being divided up on a whiteboard, and a consultancy role I had taken on after leaving the corporate world. Both the marriage and the job had gone on for too long; both had deteriorated into a toxic place to be. Surviving was a daily practice at home and at work.

The hot pink coat was one of the flashes of pink, so I wore it all the time. It was my invincibility cloak to convince myself as much as others that I was this vibrant, passionate, confident flamingo, full of life and color. I strode into the hotel reception for One of Many, looking more confident than I felt inside, and headed for the registration table to grab my lanyard. I was met with warm smiles and encouragement from the wonderful women who gave their time to support the intensives and the training. I got more than one comment that day, and for many days after. "You are the lady in pink!" It stuck and so the pink coat became more than a talisman for my confidence. It became part of my identity, and my world.

With their pink plumage, flamingos have not surprisingly featured in my home and work, showing up in my logo for a while, and people often choose gifts with a flamingo theme for me. I have pictures, plates, mugs, scarfs and even a dress with flamingo designs. I love that a group of flamingos is called a flamboyance. I have received many flamingo cards with fun messages: "We flamingo together and you are a flamingo amongst pigeons"—all a reflection of how much colour shows up in my world. I have since learned that as flamingos become mothers, they slowly lose their vibrant pink shade, becoming white as they give all the nutrients away from their food source to their young. I could see myself in that, a flamingo slowly losing her color until there was nothing left. I see this as one of those moments—one of those stars—as I look back and connect. Joining One of Many, becoming a coach, and guiding others back to their true selves—to their full color—to thrive in a life they love, became my way of bringing color back to myself, too. The touches of pink I had always been drawn to were being rediscovered, consciously and creatively.

When I came to do my first professional photo shoot for my coaching practice website, I pulled the coat on as I rushed out the door to drop the kids at school and headed to the local seaside town of Whitstable to meet my photographer, Karen. We had chosen to meet at a favorite beachside hotel, close to the beach hut a friend shared with me, which we had decided would be a perfect location for the shoot. Sharing my love for the sea and the beautiful North Kent coastline where I lived, Whitstable is famous for its oysters and the colorful beach huts that line up from the town center to the slopes at Tankerton. In my bag I had a change of clothes, a bright pink blouse to pull on over my relaxed look of a black T-shirt and blue jeans with flip-flops, because everything is better in flip-flops. Into the galaxy of potential!

The coat became the star of the show. Karen captured me on the beach, arms spread wide with the pink popping against the blue of the sea and the sky. It stood out against the dark-painted blue slats of the beach hut outside and the nautical blue and white interior. The photos and the colors would influence the creative direction of my brand, and so much more. With my marketing alchemist, Paula, who was with me that day and every day since, we matched the pink in my coat to create the unique Complement Coaching pantone color that we still use today. Several re-brands and re-creations later, the hot pink color we created from my coat remains at the very core of my brand.

After my branding shoot, I felt full of authentic confidence, embracing myself and fully tapping into my true self. Five years later, we also color-matched this to create a paint for my very own pink kitchen wall, underneath the pink was my declaration of who I am, created from my Be With session with Steve Hardison.

At the end of 2021, I had read a book called *The Ultimate Coach*, by Amy Hardison. This book was so powerful, so hypnotic, and it spoke to every part of my being. I read and listened to it countless times. The book, written about Steve Hardison, made me realize that I was destined to meet him and work with him. I wanted to create the possibility for myself to coach with him, to invest in myself and commit to giving myself that gift. What initially seemed impossible became a reality when, in January 2023, I flew over 5000 miles to Phoenix for my session with The Ultimate Coach.

During my transformative session with Steve, he quickly recognized my deep connection to the color pink. As I expressed my desire to create a new story for myself—one filled with peace, unlimited potential and authenticity—he encouraged me to write down the negative beliefs I held about myself.

As I shared those unkind thoughts, Steve listened with compassion and then invited me to reframe them. He asked, "What else is possible?" and guided me in transforming those beliefs into loving declarations. At that moment, I felt a profound shift; I no longer identified with the negativity that had weighed me down for so long.

What struck me most was when I noticed Steve wearing pink that day. It felt like a tribute to my journey and my vibrant identity. His choice to don this color in my honor reinforced the importance of embracing our authentic selves. He reminded me we are projectors of our own stories and that we can choose what we share with the world.

Leaving that session, I felt liberated and renewed. I was ready to embrace my true self and live into my highest potential. I walked in as 'the lady who wears pink' and walked out as 'Source's Pink Angel.'

This was the experience that truly illuminated the power of color for me—not just as an expression of identity but as a catalyst for transformation. Embracing pink became more than just a personal choice; it was a declaration of love, authenticity and the potential to rewrite my narrative. I realized that by embodying this vibrant hue, I could inspire others to do the same, turning our shared stories into a tapestry of hope and possibility.

Our lives are so colorful. The world is full of color, each shade rich with life and matching our true, authentic selves. Embracing it is so powerful.

The Declaration begins with "I am Source's Pink Angel." The declaration is how I create myself, a powerful set of statements that capture what the color does visually, the essence of who I am. Following that are declarations of who I will be and a life I am continuously and consciously creating for myself and those I love and support. For the time we lived in that home, I had the most vibrant pink backdrop for my client coaching calls, masterclasses and workshops, better than anything Zoom could create. It was a not-so-subtle call to action to share the hidden treasure behind the pink. I loved it when people asked me about the wall. There were so many ways I could share about the color, the paint, the stories and the stars that sparked the idea for the wall and how so much of my journey—of riches, self-discovery, and transformation—was there painted on a wall, unlocked and no longer hidden.

Writing about pink here for you has been a gift, an invitation to see just how I create my world through the energy of pink, how much potential I create for others, how they experience the world when they see my hot pink squares with powerful quotes, and how they describe the hot pink ripples, the magic they feel when we speak. Giving their experience a color allows them to be with who I am. Giving myself this color has given me permission to be who I am. Choosing a color could be the permission you need to be You.

As I have explored how pink has helped me create a love for life, and a life I love, personally and professionally, I have created a Pink Philosophy—a constellation, a thread, a way of being that I trust will light you up and guide you to see the stars connecting in your past and in your world. My invitation is to find the color in this for you. You can take the Pink philosophy as it is, or create your own with the color that lights you up, that connects you with who you are. I would love to read your colorful story sometime in my future. Nothing would bring me more joy than to know I brought a little color into your world today, and that reading this created one of those moments, those stars that become part of your constellation, shining brightly to guide you to your future self and all your hidden potential.

As the most fabulous Audrey Hepburn, a picture-perfect vision of her in pink hangs in my room so eloquently said, “I believe in pink.”

This is my belief in the Pink philosophy…

P - Purpose: Discovering my true calling and pursuing it with passion and determination.

I - Individuality: Embracing my unique strengths, talents and perspectives, and encouraging others to do the same.

N - Nurture: Cultivating an environment of support, growth and empowerment for myself and those around me.

K - Kindness: Leading with empathy, compassion and understanding, and striving to make a positive impact in the world.

Profound transformation like this only unfolds when we embrace our true selves. My journey, rooted in the vibrant energy of pink, has illuminated not just my potential but also the possibilities in those around me. Pink embodies joy, passion, and empowerment—a reminder that we can shine brightly in our uniqueness.

This vivid hue inspires us to express ourselves fully, radiating authenticity in every facet of our lives. Each time I wear my hot pink attire or surround myself with this colour, I reflect on the journey that has brought me here—a journey rich with realizations and transformative experiences.

For me, pink transcends mere color; it embodies a philosophy—a way of being that champions passion, individuality, nurture, and kindness. By sharing my story, I hope to ignite your curiosity to explore your own vibrant colors, uncovering the hidden treasures within and expressing your unique self without reservation. Just as I've discovered strength and connection through the pink thread woven into my life, I invite you to seek out your radiant hues.

As everyone who knows me would concur, I love a quote and another one springs to mind here. The wonderful Coco Chanel famously said, 'The best color in the whole world is the one that looks good on you.'

Let this chapter serve as a gentle nudge to awaken your inner light and celebrate your authenticity. Together, let's paint the world with its beautiful spectrum and create a tapestry rich in love, purpose, and limitless potential. As we embrace who we truly are, we not only uplift ourselves but also empower those around us to shine just as brightly. Join me on this journey of richness, and let's inspire one another to be gloriously, colorfully and unapologetically ourselves.

Pink is a way of being that has unlocked so much for me; it has led me to places, people, and experiences. It has revealed a depth of love and understanding for myself and others that I could not have imagined. This is expressed through ripples of hot pink that sparkle and shine, in who I am, what I wear, the people I work with and the way I show up in the world. The way I write and share stories, the way I create events and content, and following my color has led me here to this page, to this chapter, to this book and to you.

Following your color, has the potential to unlock all of this for you, too, to lead you to your hidden gold, pink, or blue. A pot so full of possibilities, it is there for you all the while at the end of your rainbow. Life is a journey, and sometimes the most significant transformations begin when we remember to believe in ourselves and when we remember to embrace our inner light, our inner color.

It is there, it may just be a little hidden. Like the beautiful flamingo, we may have lost our color, our true selves, for a while. Lost in the day-to-day dealings of life, or lives we find ourselves in as we journey through them without much awareness, unconsciously hiding who we are. If you are reading this, my wish for you is that this is the glimmer, the sparkle, and the shine that permits you to be gloriously, colorfully, fabulously, and authentically you.

Be the brightest blue, the poppiest red, the tangiest orange, the most nurturing green, or the warmest of yellows. Be the sunshine, the ocean, the sky, or the forest. Be a vibrant flamingo or a beautiful white swan. Or perhaps you are a hot pink swan—be creative, unique, and most of all, be you. There is so much potential hidden in your unique and authentic color.

“Believe you can and you're halfway there.”

~ Theodore Roosevelt

CHAPTER THREE

From Hidden Pain to Hidden Potential

By Cari Rickabaugh

Like it happened yesterday, I remember hearing my voice say the words loud and clear in my head, spoken slowly because it was difficult to actually believe *"I Have Potential."* It was as if a light bulb suddenly clicked in my brain and an understanding that I had never known set in. A feeling started filling my body that was completely foreign—a peace that seemed to permeate every cell within me. This wasn't necessarily happiness, but a sense of calmness that my nervous system had never experienced. It was as if my soul was saying, "Finally, Cari. You finally *get* it." I remember hoping that I could hold on to that feeling forever…

I had been told my entire life, "You have so much potential," but I never knew what that meant. Other people could see it in me, but I never could. Even after figuring out what "it" meant, I still couldn't fully grasp that I had it. What I didn't know was that I couldn't yet see it. There were so many walls that were in front of me (metaphorically) that there was no way I could see beyond who I was being currently to the possibility of being or doing *anything* different. Who I was being was the same version of me I had been for twenty years.

Let me jump back a few decades to explain why this was. Growing up in my home was less than pleasant. On the outside we looked like the ideal family—both parents in the home, three kids still at home plus one living out of state, a dog, a modest house, a pool, three vehicles, etc. Nothing above or below average. But behind closed doors, it was a different story. There were rules we functioned by…unspoken rules:

- Always *act* as if everything is ok.
- Do what 'looks good' in front of others—appearances are *everything.*
- *Never* ask questions.
- Don't rock the boat or else.
- Emotions and needs are selfish and must be repressed.
- Only positive feelings are acceptable.
- Do as I say, not as I do.
- Submission is demanded.

This created role-players and actors. It meant that not only could I never be authentically myself, I also never knew who I was. I had vague ideas about things I liked and disliked, but I never could bring myself to decide for fear of it being "wrong." Talk about the ideal environment to suppress one's unlimited potential!

There was also abuse on every level: mental, emotional, physical. I learned how to gauge the potential for abuse at any moment by the way someone sighed or the weight of their steps. Every mistake created extreme fear because the expectation was perfection in everything (without being taught anything), so there was discipline given and no grace for being human. Every door closing or creak of the hallway hardwood floor brought a rush of fear. There was no safe space to retreat to. Maybe you can relate to this kind of scenario in your home.

I think it's helpful to pause now and consider what potential is and how it contradicts my upbringing. Based upon multiple definitions, potential can include the inherent ability or capacity within someone to achieve, develop, or become something greater in the future. We can define potential as what someone could achieve or realize under the right conditions, even if it isn't currently clear or fully expressed. Practice, opportunity, or growth reveals a person's potential talents, capabilities, or skills. It represents the possibility of change, development, and achievement.

Growing up in conditions that didn't allow me to create myself programmed me to be only what I had been told I was. Moving out after high school, I continued living life as the only version of me I thought was possible. This created a lot of difficulties and hardships. I didn't get along with people or roommates very well, especially those who were emotionally mature and mentally healthy. Considering any option or opinion that differed from mine was difficult or impossible to accept. Moreover, I only knew how to extend conditional love, as long as someone fit inside my box of arbitrary "rules" that were worthy of me. However, everyone was worthy of my condemnation—*that* I knew how to give out freely.

I believed the ways I functioned were set in stone and couldn't be altered. I had never really developed a personality, so I thought that things only happened *to* me. I did not know I could make decisions that would change the things I didn't like in my life. When the universe was handing out difficulties, I felt I had more than my share, and I just learned to "white-knuckle" through the suffering. I figured if that's all I was going to be given in life, then I would be suffering until the day I died…and assumed it was that way because I deserved it.

Those ways of thinking did not allow for my potential to be reached or even considered. I did not know I could become something greater. I couldn't comprehend that I could choose the outcome of my life. To many, that would sound ludicrous, but it was my reality. To find hidden potential, one has to look for it. I had metaphorical blinders on and could only see what was on the path directly in front of me—which were the same and only things that I had ever known…who I had been told that I was. "Hidden" is the keyword here. It must be searched for and sought after. You must do things differently than you have ever done before, and I didn't have that ability. Making choices for myself was completely outside of my scope of understanding.

Joyce Meyer once said, "Potential is a priceless treasure, like gold. All of us have gold hidden within, but we have to dig to get it out." Now, I believe this practice of "digging" requires multiple things: willingness, the proper tools, and support from others who have dug into their potential. Without those three things collectively, it's often difficult—if not impossible—to know where and how to dig.

So, how did I discover my potential? Let me tell you a story….

I have a dear friend that I met when we were both in our very early twenties. Eric and I bonded quickly, and I was lucky to help and support him as he changed his life. A couple of years later, Eric got married and moved out of state. We didn't see each other again for the next eighteen years. When we finally met up again, I realized that he had matured while I had stayed the same 22-year-old I was when we met. I had tried over those years to change so many things about myself but had failed at every turn. I couldn't lose the "me" that I'd always known, the version of myself that others had created by telling me who I was, the "me" that was only made up of mistakes and failures.

Over the next few years, I sought help in therapy to learn how to work through the thirty years of trauma that started when I was twelve, which I knew was part of the problem and needed to be addressed. I sought out three different therapists, each of whom quickly told me only a few minutes into telling them why I was there that there was an "easy answer" to healing my specific trauma and that I should be fine and "done with needing therapy" in twelve weeks. Twelve weeks?! Only three months?! The simple answer from each of them was to re-parent myself.

I had no idea what this meant, and none of them could explain to me *how* to do it; it was just what they kept telling me to do. Nothing got resolved or processed, so each time we got to the twelfth session, they each said, "You should be good now," and shooed me out of their office. By the third time this happened I fully believed that I was too broken to be helped. Reaching my full potential seemed like an impossible mirage reserved for anyone but me.

When you think you've hit rock bottom but keep finding that your rock bottom has a basement, you feel as if there is no way you can ever climb out. Over the next few years, I became more and more bitter and depressed. I felt that I couldn't make any progress, and trying to function in the "truth" that "I sucked as a human being" ate away at my limited potential a little more every day. I eventually developed multiple auto-immune issues, living in constant physical pain, and spent most of every day in bed. It felt like my friends started falling away, too, because this version of me wasn't very pleasant to be around and I was physically very needy. It was just too much.

At this point, my suicidal ideation, which started when I was thirteen, began to run rampant again. I eventually made a plan that I'm glad didn't pan out. No one knew I was about to walk off a metaphorical ledge that there was no returning from. In my mind, all those people who had told me I had potential were completely wrong. I believed I was nothing more than who I was existing as at that moment.

A few days before following through on that plan, I received a random call from Eric, wanting to introduce me to his friend Dave, who was a life coach. This completely caught me off guard, and it was confusing for him as well. Later, I learned Eric had been getting a *really* strong feeling that this needed to happen and that he needed to do whatever it took to make sure this happened *right away*. He couldn't understand why, as he didn't know how bad my depression had gotten, or what I was planning. He was the lifeline that I needed. That call ended up saving my life and becoming the catalyst to finding out who I was, and that I truly did have potential.

Dave was this incredibly kind man who, through Neuro Linguistic Programming and his unorthodox method, took me back into my trauma and *taught me* what re-parenting was. For me, this truly was the magic elixir that helped release the past and walk into reaching my unlimited potential. His style worked with how my mind could go back and process all those memories I had hanging over me since I was twelve.

I started to feel myself healing and changing. Between our sessions, I worked on the skills and processes that Dave had been teaching me, and I even sometimes came to the next week's session, having worked through something completely on my own. My auto-immune issues were receding. I didn't feel as dark and heavy inside anymore, and how I was thinking about myself was surprising even to me! I can't even begin to fully express how that felt when I had come from such a place of hopelessness in ever being able to be different. In my mind, I was advancing in a linear stream, and life would soon be all rainbows and unicorns, as soon as I had "worked through" all those memories.

But life rarely ever works how we think it will.

Dave and I spent the next eight or nine months working through those thirty-plus years of trauma. Around that time, he suggested we work on the creation of what I wanted the rest of my life to comprise, as there wasn't much that was still surfacing for me to work through anymore. Oh, there were small things here and there, but nothing that I felt I couldn't handle on my own. Yet I kept telling him no, that it wasn't time yet. I had this strange feeling within me. We kept meeting weekly, but we were kind of in limbo for the next four weeks.

What happened next is still unbelievable to me when I think about it.

A few months before this, my body had begun having physical releases. In my twenties, I often had unexplained seizures (that were later linked to the trauma), so I knew these releases weren't seizures. I resisted them every time they happened out of fear. I tried to control them to keep them from happening, but I couldn't. Finally, I accepted them and relinquished my attempts to control the outcome. With that relinquishment of control, the other memories clouding my sense of potential started flooding back.

The first time I remember it happening I was probably about five years old, but it had been happening since long before I could remember. I would wake up to him pushing my nightgown up and pulling my underwear off. The panic alarm in my head would go off, and I would immediately be in the depths of a 'freeze' state. I wanted to scream "STOP!" and kick him away, but I knew that wasn't an option. Submission was the unspoken rule.

In all honesty, I didn't know this was wrong, I just knew that it was something that I dreaded. You mean, this doesn't happen to every child? The unspoken rules were always in play: 'Never ask questions,' 'Always act as if everything is ok,' 'Do as I say, not as I do.' There was nothing I could do about it. Every time I just had to wait until it was over.

As the years went on, the sexual abuse got worse, and there was mental abuse intertwined with it. When I was seven, I had an experience in which a family member walked in on a friend and me playing. They thought we were doing something sexual, even though we weren't. They took me to another room, claimed God was angry with me and didn't love me because I was involved in sexual activities, and forced me to pray and repent. I was told the words to say, and as this went on, I felt incredibly nauseous. After I said “Amen,” they asked me how I felt. “Like I’m going to throw up,” I weakly replied. I was told, “See, that’s the Holy Ghost confirming that God is angry at you for participating in these things.” I ran to the bathroom and started dry heaving. Once that stopped, I was told, “Ok, go back and play with your friend now!” No one ever mentioned it again. The concept of me having unlimited potential and that anything was possible was never a topic of conversation.

I realized that was the moment I internalized the belief that I was worthless. I mean, I had been taught that God loves everyone, even murderers! So all my seven-year-old brain could comprehend was that God loved every person who ever lived on this planet…except for me. I was too young to realize that you can’t always believe everything that is told to you by people who are never supposed to lie to you. If God didn’t love me because of something sexual that hadn’t happened with my friend, then He must hate me for the things that *were* happening *to* me. When you believe that, then every time another night of abuse happens, every time I froze and didn’t push him away, that “truth” was imprinted even deeper.

The last incident of sexual abuse was so extreme that I finally told a family member. When I said, “There was a man in my room last night!” I imagined they would run to me and wrap me in a hug of love so tight that it would make everything Ok, and would say, “I’ll never let anyone hurt you again!” What actually happened was, they said, “Don’t worry about it!” and then turned around and walked out the door.

I was ten years old. I didn't know what to do. The unspoken rules were again in play: "Emotions and needs are selfish and must be repressed," "Only positive feelings are acceptable," "Don't rock the boat, or else." It was in this moment that I 'realized' that no one cared enough to protect me, and I would have to do it myself.

I immediately started building massive invisible walls around myself to keep *everyone* at bay, and then also forced myself to forget that I was doing that; it just became a part of how I functioned. I also started forgetting almost everything related to the sexual abuse. I have always remembered a few flashes from that last night, but nothing that I could put together to make sense of. I started burying all the sexual abuse and anything related to it so deep inside of me, I couldn't access it. I would often be triggered throughout my life because of it, but I never knew what was happening or why.

In some ways, I was stuck in the ages of when those things happened. My maturity was halted, and therefore I struggled so greatly to change anything about myself. When a different form of abuse started at age thirteen, which my mind allowed me to remember, it was piled on top of the buried memories of abuse. This buried my potential. It truly became hidden. So when I had worked through most of the known trauma to where Dave felt we could start to move forward, I had no idea that there was another decade of trauma left to uncover. My body knew though, and that's why it kept telling me it wasn't time yet.

Once these memories started coming back, Dave and I worked on accepting, processing, and releasing them. But even through all of this, I just could not wrap my head around the fact that I had anything to offer this world or that I could do much right other than the occasional thing here or there. Dave tried to help me create things for my life and start to see my potential, but the wall I built as a child remained, preventing me from accepting the truth that I had potential, that I had any worth, or that I could create anything new in my life.

During this time I had a conversation with my friend Tony. There was a conference I wanted to attend on the other side of the country, but I "knew" there was no way I could make attending it work (because I fully believed that I wasn't worth anything good happening for me). Tony somehow convinced me I could and needed to do it. Long story short, I ended up getting tickets to the event and flight and found a place to stay the next day, and four days later, I was flying out to this conference. I was functioning on his belief in me and *his* vision for my potential.

When I got to the conference the night before to help set up, everything seemed to go wrong. I was making one mistake after another, and I didn't know how to deal with that in front of a group of people that I barely knew, none of whom I had ever met in person before. I still was unconsciously functioning under the impression that perfection was the only acceptable way to be. I ended up hiding in the bathroom bawling after just a couple hours, wishing I had never come, trying to figure out some way that I could quickly get back on a plane home, and feeling completely hopeless that all the work I had done over the previous then almost a year was all for naught. I was convinced that I would always be a failure and a screw-up.

After a while, I gathered myself, splashed water on my face, and went back into the venue. I meandered around, trying to put on a happy face and trying not to touch anything or say much to anyone, all the while wondering why in the world I had ever believed that this time I could differ from the way I had always been.

Eventually, all of us there (probably thirty-five people) gathered in a circle to say a prayer and dedicate the venue for the conference. After the prayer, the person in charge informed us we would have a few minutes to connect and reflect before gathering together again.

I wanted to explore every part of the room because I knew from the next day onwards, I would be assigned to a table and spend most of the conference in that area. I walked in between the tables, trying to take in everything from every angle. Eventually, I ended up at the far side of the room and just stood to watch everything else that was going on in front of me. One person was sitting cross-legged on the stage, with their face in their hands, crying. Others were walking around the tables, hugging each other. A few people were alone in their own worlds, offering prayers or blessings. One person was smudging the surrounding people. Some, like myself, stood in various places around the perimeter of the room, also watching the scene unfold. Tears were present for many. Love was abundant and could be felt in the air. The music was moving and added to the rise of emotions and energy in the room. I hadn't ever experienced anything quite like this before, and I could now consider myself blessed to be in that room and a part of that experience.

I was so entranced in what I watched I didn't notice three men suddenly surrounded me—two I had just met and one I didn't know at all. It happened so quickly and unexpectedly that I didn't have time to put up my invisible walls to keep myself from getting "hurt." These men embraced me in a hug of love and safety that was so powerful it destroyed every single wall that I had put up regarding my worth. This was the hug that I had needed when I was ten. I again started sobbing as their energy carried me to let go of the beliefs that I had been taught in my youth. This was the moment that everything changed for me. It was in that instant that tapping into my potential became a possibility. I suddenly knew that I was enough and knew why I was at that conference: to find out who I *really* was.

Those men and that memory will always hold a deep place in my heart, and I will remember it as the moment I was shifted to finally understand and believe what others had so often told me: *"I Have Potential.*"

"Your potential is unlocked when you step outside your comfort zone and take bold steps toward your goals."

~ Stephen Covey

CHAPTER FOUR

Entering The Cave...

By Ben Welch

If I didn't begin this chapter by telling you about the intense level of fear I hold—even at the very idea of writing something that enters the world to be read and judged by anyone and everyone—you wouldn't fully understand the journey I've been on and where I'm coming from to speak of hidden potential.

I grew up feeling and believing I was dumb. Confronting that belief now, I don't even know why I would think that was true. I was told my whole life that my writing was lousy; I received poor grades in school, except for physical education and math. Looking back, I can see that my limiting beliefs about who I was matched the distraction and lack of effort I applied to school, which I perceived as a waste of time. Yet, the thing I've noticed most since finishing school is how much I love learning. I've never stopped. I've embraced new opportunities time after time. While I often thought my greatest fear was failing, I've spent some time now reflecting with wonder and curiosity and realizing that my greatest fear may have actually been succeeding. I notice it's the possibility of our hidden potential that scares us the most.

Each time I choose to expand my potential and truly go All In. I transform my human *being*—or, as has become even more apparent to me, my human *experiencing.*

Different applications of energy create distinct feelings, which lead to different experiences and, ultimately, a different life.

In exploring the idea of hidden potential, I learned how the word "Is" represents creation.

When you or I say something "Is" it becomes something for us, we create by it; it manifests into our personal reality through the spell of *meaning* we declared and becomes an energy state within us.

For example, it literally took me until the eleventh hour to join the others in writing chapters for this book. This hesitation stemmed from fear. Patterns of procrastination embedded in my psyche, and the belief in the false narrative that anything I wrote couldn't possibly be valid alongside the work of these other amazing contributors.

This is the thing about hidden potential, though, isn't it? The only things hidden are those we choose not to look at or confront…

A favorite quote of my coach that has now become one of my own is from American mythologist Joseph Campbell:

"The cave we fear to enter holds the treasure that we seek."

This is where our highest potential lives and going *into and through* the darkness is the only path to get there.

What is hidden remains hidden by choice because All is available. We have unlimited access to information via the internet or our imaginations. Nothing is inaccessible to the human mind—only focus and choice make it so.

According to the Oxford Languages dictionary, the definition of "potential" in physics is: *the quantity determining the energy of mass in a gravitational field or of charge in an electric field.*

Each human being is an electric field. A human being—whether you or I—through awareness, choice, thought, and focus, can create "a change in gravitational potential, a change in human *being*."

Potential has always been present in human beings. Who we become along life's path has more to discover and create when we approach life with courage. For me, courage is the secret sauce to flavor life.

Every perceived risk or limitation that *we give permission* to possess our minds and define our narrative of what we are limited to being and doing becomes a new stumbling block, stunting all that is potentially available to us. However, if we choose to confront these fears—to stand with courage and open arms to whatever outcomes we may translate as life—we unlock opportunities for hidden potential. I propose that this space and point of creation, "I Am"—is where hidden potential resides. Not the "I am" you say over and over out loud to try to make yourself do or be something, the 'I am' you declare in your mind from belief and your choice most of the time unconsciously.

This is not a weak statement of saying "I Am…" over and over. This is a believing with a conception moment of the permission we give for what we decide to experience as "I Am." This statement when embodied, gives energy permission to enter our body and *become*, create a change as a force that makes our life what *we* say it is—this is *meaning* and beginning of creation.

Do you notice how, from the statement above, hidden potential conceptually feels like something 'somewhere'—like a space inside us?

When I first sat down to write this chapter, I immediately recalled Jordan Peterson speaking about how to write a book. What I understood him to say was:

"To write a book, we must begin with the best question one can find and go on a discovery voyage into the potential hidden inside."

To uncover the gold in this incredible idea, we must be the human who dares to openly even consider what is possible (which is harder than we may sometimes think) and then *do* the things we have feared before. In my fear, I am seizing this moment with both hands and embarking on a journey into myself and perhaps you will explore inside yourself, too. Becoming open, vulnerable and courageous as we will uncover are the pathways to and through our hearts, the discovery of inner truth and recognition of our Self rather than the adoption of external implication and validation and identification with the ego mind.

I love the fact that power is available to each of us to expand, because we are the question, the limitations and the answers, all wrapped in the beautiful, adventurous and miraculous package of "human being."

The best question I found for me and us for this book's theme is: “How is it possible for our potential to get hidden, and where would we go looking?”

It turns out that a very significant moment of personal growth along my journey of life might be part of the answer.

Let's examine the idea closely together.

It wasn’t in a coaching session or a deep personal reflection; it wasn’t in journaling or even the often-challenging reflection of a loved one, as with most of the gold of life. It hid in a moment of presence and awareness to frustration and anger—a moment by chance on the squash court.

While being rather competitive with sports about ten years ago and I was playing against my highly competitive friend. I’m sure you can imagine the banter and the pain of being ten points down and repeatedly beaten at each point by virtually the same shot for several games. To say I was fuming would be a vast understatement of the internal experience I was creating.

As he was about to win again, Nick, my Zimbabwean opponent, offered me a moment of mercy. While I’d like to propose that he is a purely kind and graceful guy, that wouldn’t be true. This mercy came with the most infuriating thing for a man being beaten so convincingly—and something Nick really loved—an even greater reason to gloat!

“Do you know why I keep beating you with that shot?” he asked.

“No,” I replied, somewhat frustrated—or, some might say, peaking with the pressure of a suppressed volcanic eruption.

"You've got a blind spot, mate," came the reply in that bordering arrogant yet calm-toned Zimbabwean/English/Aussie mixed-up accent Nick has rarely moved from.

He asked, "Would you like me to show you?"

Noticing this trigger I had, that as my ego rose inside wanting to tell Nick where he could jam my "blind spot," the open, more emotionally mature part of me responded with a surprisingly receptive, "Yes, please."

As he pointed to a spot on the wall—although a little higher—it was similarly positioned to the place where, while driving your car, you cannot see in any of your mirrors. You know, just over the shoulder, behind your ear, just into that space where it would take some effort and a second longer to catch that squash ball landing, and like the passing car, as you pull in front of it, it so rudely beeps to interrupt your moment of simple obliviousness to what was actually occurring in reality. This displays how our perception can sometimes be tricked by our own mind, by untruths that exist inside our beliefs and then repeatedly create unwanted results.

Growing up with the highly suppressing and strict beliefs of a cult, being manipulated into my perceptions through fear, all hidden under the guise of love. All life choices were made under pressure, limitation, and fear. These things I gave permission to create me, by matching the events of life to meanings about who I am, or rather, who I was. Most of all, the hurtful belief and blind spot that I needed something or someone external to validate my amazing and beautiful internal being that had existed from the moment of my conception into the mind and reality of Life.

My potential was hidden until I became aware of the triggers and blind spots that were hiding in me, maybe even—locked away?

Fortunately, this moment on the squash court uncovered a new viewpoint on life.

With this awareness I deliberately turned inward to become the observer of the blind spots, immediately accessing opportunities to transform hurt into joy and problems into solutions, automatically discovering hidden levels of potential.

I propose, regarding this example, that it's not that we are too lazy to turn and see it—it's more likely that there is a fear of looking, of really seeing, and of **knowing**. An inhibition or an existing story about what we'll see if we face the shame, the rage or anger - or - the shame of the rage and anger we might uncover in ourselves at having held back from fully living life. For many years of my life, it was most definitely that for me. What I've discovered about this topic is that I have found so much power in seeing more truth about myself, rather than *what is true and real available information.* The permission and power I have often unknowingly given the story inside ***to overtake me***, which I assert is the true source of the fear. The story doesn't want to be seen. The story creates the untrue experience, or as I like to call it, the *trick* of stuck-ness. I've now caught that the greatest fear is that I have the power to see it, know it, and our capacity is fully available to *change it.*

Knowing ourselves is the ultimate freedom and inside us the best space to plant a new story seed that sets us on course to *expose and realize* our potential.

Approximately two years before this blind spot story, I had changed careers. By the force and necessity of pain in my body—represented metaphorically above by Nick and losing—I now see I benefited from discovering awareness of yet another blind spot. This revealed significant hidden potential that I, and any human being, could majorly benefit from expanding: purposely gaining physical strength.

In my 20s, I had been in construction for about eight years, suffering from what became chronic back pain, plus hip pain, knee pain, neck pain, headaches, and fortnightly or monthly migraines. I was physically a mess. Unable to sit up after waking in bed, and had to roll onto my knees before slowly and gingerly making my way around the pinching nerves to a standing position. I followed this with my morning ritual of lying on hot wheat bags to loosen my back.

Thinking my work life and a car accident earlier in life had caused this, but as it became too much to bear, I learned to enter the cave of the partial fear "I Am this pain." My actual cave was the question—and still a fear—"Who would I be without pain?"

The courage and treasure in the chests (also known as questions) - "How does my body work?"

And "What opportunities were there for me to heal myself?"

Hmm, do you notice the curiosity and openness to hidden potential in that question?

By becoming open to just one question, rather than blindly believing in the fifteen years of pain I had endured, a plethora of new and amazing knowledge and awareness suddenly became available. I observed what was 'actually happening' as I moved through life in the physical sense.

Would we call this facing reality?

Dropping resistance to what *is*?

Dropping resistance to what might differ from what we have labeled and believed something to be?

I learned very quickly a principle statement that can cover all of life's limitations:

Tightness = Weakness

Any tightness stopping us from expanding reflects a weakness, which is not a problem, only flags an opportunity for strength, and it turns out.

Strength = Flexibility and mobility

I became focused on moving freely and feeling strong. Similarly to the squash game, with new awareness, I switched approach from defending against the pain or the shot Nick was hitting to instead attacking the ball committed and *all in*. At the very least, I placed myself in a situation of continuing to compete and learn a new place to come *from*.

In the gym, one step at a time, I attacked every fear of pain with a faith that held certainty that my body could and would become whole, strong, and pain-free. As my strength increased, so did my flexibility, mobility, and capacity to move without fear. This also led to my ability to see, technically, the physical blind spots of others. The tightness from weakness that were creating pain. With the study required, I learned to describe and prescribe the movements and processes, enabling me to invite my clients to discover their potential "through" the blind spots of their pain.

Hidden potential uncovered and unlocked, right?

Faced fear → Healed pain → Freedom and new energy available for something else.

Increased personal power and a new vision and idea of myself = Identity Transformation.

That's an uncovered and unlocked treasure chest available to all!

All from one moment of choice and commitment—now that is curious, isn't it?

It turns out that, after waiting for pain to force me toward power in many areas, hidden potential isn't such a difficult thing to discover. The capacity to see it, Be it, and do its required actions—or maybe first just catch a glimpse of what's in one's blind spots—is key. Even more amazing, we don't *have* to wait for pain to bring us to this! There is a little disclaimer here, though: one must be *open* to the awareness that it exists to see potential for transformation. The actual availability for that would be in direct correlation to our capacity to remain open in uncertainty (also known as vulnerability). While I see action as the physical door to our hidden potential, I believe one hundred percent that remaining open in the face of uncertainty is the *key* to it!

One of my teachers and mentors, Joe Pane, says, "Emotional fitness is measured by the quality of our relationships with uncertainty."

When we are flexible with our emotional fitness, we can access higher levels of potential. This is more like it - short, concise and to the point.

Until a specific point in my life, I believed and so *was* entirely unable to *be with* and by that, I mean allow myself to feel the uncertainty of the hidden potential of my emotions.

Do you recall that moment in the squash match when I considered telling Nick what to do with his observation of my weakness? Life challenges us to stay open in faith and realize that we are internally stronger and more powerful than any challenge we could ever face.

Frederick Nietzsche wrote, "Until you make the unconscious conscious, it will direct your life and you will call it fate."

An internal giant, we are full of potential. This potential is only covered over by conditioned learning that became unconscious. Given meanings, we end up believing and calling 'truth', keeping us a small and limited person of our own making. Our job is to have the emotional strength and courage to go in the dark, bring it forward and make it conscious.

Human beings, whether we like it or not, bring their emotional state into the world in every moment of life, *as life*—we, in each moment, Are It.

Think about your experience of life right now, receiving the words I am writing. You feel something upon the judgment (perspective coming from fear) or discernment (perspective coming from love) of my words, and we are bringing ourselves into the world, translating from one of those energetic spaces inside. We are a *being* who is read subconsciously by others even before any words leave our mouth. Words often only confirm what others feel about us before we speak. Most people remain unaware that, in an even greater way than their thoughts run their lives, their bodies are reacting unconsciously and habitually to emotional programs we created by agreement, often in childhood, without full understanding.

These agreements are adopted by reacting in the blink of an eye before conscious thought can choose a desired response and research has since found that a simple _pause_ is enough to significantly change our reactions to newly chosen responses.

Responding is often lost to humans because these programs hide in the dark; the habitual reaction is standard for most. These programs are things we fear facing or changing because they demand an identity shift and change. *Who knows how the healed pain and uncovered power will change us?* Essentially, the cave of unknown potential is a scary place to enter.

In the pretty standard 1980s to 1990s male manner, my upbringing taught me not to cry, or I'd be given something to cry about. Not to be too sensitive because sensitivity was considered a weakness and a source of humor to my father (perhaps a reflection for him?)

Taught by many men: don’t be emotional because emotions would make me weak, take me over, and turn me into a sinful, lusting backslider from the beliefs of the system I was raised in. Emotions, they warned, would lead me straight to a burning lake of fire in hell for the uncontrolled behaviors that would most certainly result. And yet, even as a child, I could see the hypocrisy of their actions, the fear they lived by, and how crippling it was to their lives and potential. Still, I believed the fear—and it became the padlock on the treasure chest of my potential in the many caves I feared to even peer into, let alone enter.

This became the ultimate blind spot for me.

Many caves of darkness I deeply feared to enter. Places where all my greatest hidden potential became the pressure cooker that created a hellish experience every day for thirty years or more because I still am uncovering them now at 44. A place where between 22 and 27 years old, death seemed like the ideal answer, and thinking about it was a pattern that owned me; even though in the real circumstances of life, things were great, it was totally illogical - a blind spot, right? The place in my mind where I would lose all the games of life until I reached enough pain in the throes of ending mine because of this internal suffering, pain, inner rage, and anger, I only really wanted to end the story of myself. That was when what seemed like my most inner voice quietly whispered—but I just wanted to fully live—*and in that moment, a blink of an eye, I transformed.*

The pain of a life not fully lived suddenly became the reason to confront the darkness, to face a blind spot of pain, to willingly sit and spend time with emotions and fears that had owned me, even without making sense. In the same way I had overcome pain and weakness to change physically, I began the adventure and discovered how emotional pain was hiding potential.

As a man married for twenty-four years who has had five children (four of whom are living), I have transformed the depths of depression from the loss of a son; I was emotionally stunted and unable to grieve, to where I went into the dark, *through* grief and discovered more love than I would ever have believed was possible. Not from external sources, *and* rather from the pit of myself.

I grew up part of a family and community where fear was the catalyst for teaching behavior, discipline, and control with the threat of death and imagined hell as the outcome of disobedience. A little cultish maybe?

As a child I bought those patterns of belief and thinking, because each time I went against them by my focus on the fear of being wrong, I proved what I was told, which resulted in a terrified experience within. Not because the experience was true, but because I subconsciously was looking to prove it to myself. Then the actions I took, unknowingly cemented a story about 'me.'

Only upon recognition that this habitual narrative that lived inside and taunted me, was a cave in a dark corner of my mind, I discovered a reservoir of hidden human potential filled with:

"You are useless."
"You don't deserve anything."
"Of course, you're a failure."
"Your family is better off without you."

And the clincher - "I am not enough."

These narratives, so deeply ingrained, had been hidden yet spoken internally often. I didn't see or hear them, and I had undoubtedly numbed myself to their feeling.

The screaming voice of my ego sounded eerily familiar, like a significant man in my life. This voice blocked out any other that might even suggest I had hidden potential. Because, after all, who would I even be if I wasn't the grief-ridden volcano of pressured lava, that came bursting out my sides, burning and scalding those closest to me—especially those I loved the most?

I can now see where I leaped off the cliff of a fixed belief system identity, who—'I believed I was'—things I repeated a million times in paranoia that "I Am" that had led me to entertain suicidal ideation as the answer to my emotional pain. I stood on the ledge of a balcony at the age of 27 for the fifth time in five years, committed to the end, *finally* uncovering the lies in those beliefs. Now, as a man who sits here writing this chapter of a book, I know the power to forgive the failure of giving in, the fear of owning Being Me, and the ability and courage to stare into and go through the blind spots of fear that have held me back in infinite ways over 44 years of life.

In conclusion of my observations and experiences and testing the hypothesis I had about unlocking our hidden potential, I want to declare what I now believe is currently Truth for me.

One's inability to first *be* with one's emotions (commonly grief or shame), when coupled with the fear of confronting the unknown darkness of some cave we know *must* be entered, often creates significant uncertainty of change. The fear of success, even at a 'small thing' that is pursued, creates a significant identity shift in a human.

I perceive that a source point of energy inside us holds our hidden potential. This is where the force that makes us wake up each day and keeps our hearts beating resides. This place to draw on is available to us in any and every moment, and it holds opportunities that match the moment of life, no matter which paths we chose before it.

The moment I stayed open and agreed to see and understand the point of the blind spot on the squash court wall—while it was 'only sport'—that pain point in my life instantly vanished. Now, I could address the issue, which gave me the power to stay in the game.

I see the metaphorical opportunity we are offered every time Life brings our attention to a blind spot. It's not always because we are incapable of turning our heads to see—it's sometimes because it didn't occur to us that it was there.

Dare we enter the cave, wherein lies the treasure chest to which we all now hold the key?

Being open to the truth that while we *are* rage, anger and grief, that we can also be the power of love and light, which shine a torch on those aspects hiding our potential.

We *are* the torch that enters the cave, holding the keys of vulnerability, courage, and openness in the face of all uncertainty, to unlock all the potential you wish to create for yourself. We have everything we need to live this life to the fullest. By being ourselves and discovering who we are through the pathways of our heart to know truth, love and power, or rage and fear. The opportunity of consciously and presently being, we can inspire and bless others in abundance of the whole that we are.

Do we have hidden potential?

I have seen, heard and feel a confirmed *yes.*

Do we have the key to the lock on the treasure chest it is in?

I believe we've discovered another *yes.*

Do we have the power to bring it to life?

In courage and vulnerability, absolutely!

In writing this chapter, I have offered love and power to you and myself. Through all our rage, or perhaps through our suppression—we are the permanent and perfect opportunity to expand more of the hidden potential that calls us forward to a new place each day and that feels more and more like home. Go In – Be Free.

“The key to unlocking your potential lies in your willingness to grow and adapt.”

~ John C. Maxwell

CHAPTER FIVE

Let the Fur Fly to Unlock Your Potential

By Corrina Bowcott

When we think of the freedom and innocence of our childhood, it brings us back to a time reminiscent of purity, a time when our inner potential is fresh and raw in our surroundings. It's when we feel the most authentic and excited to bring our passions alive. Every human being is born with inner potential. We can see and feel the energy of underexposed potential everywhere. Unfortunately, society numbs us when we haven't had the proper tools and support to reveal our golden star. Through my humble beginnings, I knew I had the potential to do grand things, but my environment stifled me and I had to set off on a journey to re-ignite my inner potential.

It all began with the music of the Beach Boys playing in the background and a content smile. Overwhelming thoughts of the possibilities in my life buzzed through my head. Awards for excellence in fitness and progressing in my musical talents were the next steps to my future of entrepreneurism. An unwavering belief that I could succeed in anything I did was at the forefront of my life. I remember saying to my peers, "Just push and you will get it."

This spiritual journey was filled with many joyous and challenging experiences. My belief system was harnessed in my eccentric little shed outside my family home. Who would have thought an old chicken coop could be a space of great insight? The countless hours spent there and in other homemade forts was where I would sit and visualize my world. Hundreds of books were consumed to create a new belief system. I spent hours upon hours in meditative daydreaming to escape from the reality of family dynamics. It was a world filled with potential and hope for the future.

The hours spent exploring and living off-grid as a young girl was another factor that leaned me into my pure hidden energy. I lived on a remote island every summer and every weekend during school. This is where I felt peace and could tap into my potential. Off-grid living was also a gift to my hidden musical talent. Not being impacted as much by society and family trauma, this was where my childhood potential was at its peak.

Having these opportunities in my life helped me forget about my home life, riddled with denial and abuse. Many times, I heard conversations in my childhood that to this day no one has talked about. These lies and denial led me to a path of discovering my full potential. I was intuitive from a young age and knew the path my family was on wasn't parallel to mine.

My intuitive abilities and belief in myself were beyond the average child, unfortunately, family dynamics worked to slowly disintegrate my belief system to the point it was hard to keep beliefs alive. When a young child is told, "You will never do anything," it is a hook that will remain in your psyche forever. My main belief is work hard and you can achieve anything, but it stayed dormant until I was well into adulthood. There were numerous attempts to bring it to the surface, but its brief appearances would be abolished by my subconscious, ego, and societal pressure. After surviving lung cancer as a 24-year-old and receiving a book on my bed called *The Miracle of Life,* I realized I was being guided to find my inner potential again. Maybe it was just because I was told I had a twenty percent chance to live, but I truly began to believe again that I was here for a reason.

Many years later, I experienced domestic violence while raising my three young children. It was a blessing and tragedy, as it was the main catalyst to bring my belief system alive again. Before this occurred, I was on my way back to my belief system and trying to light a fire on my potential. Of course, things happen in threes, and I was in a tragic head-on collision with a drunk driver. These three events were the catalyst to revive my inner belief system. I was grateful to be alive and knew I had to unleash the locked potential buried beneath the traumas. Your beliefs about yourself, your family, and the world are one of the keys to releasing your potential into the world.

Beliefs, visualizations, stepping out of my comfort zone, and exploring unique strategies in my childhood brought me to crack open my hidden potential in my adulthood and my future as an entrepreneur in the pet grooming industry.

Working hard to start a business when you are a single parent of three young children is nothing more than daunting to the average human. I never once doubted my ability to create this for my family. The beginnings of my pet grooming vision initially started with my love for animals and a desire for income to raise my three children alone and give them a good role model. At every step, I kept telling myself: "I can do this." There were many days I wanted to quit and succumb to my corporate management job in a pet grooming salon. Easily, this could have been the end of the road, but my first attempt at a pet grooming salon took shape by late-night planning while my children were asleep. I could feel my inner power and potential coming to the surface as the energy was flowing. My belief system was magically being repaired by uncovering the raging potential I had all along.

Hours upon hours of frustration and hope led me to my first grooming salon. Working a full-time job and building out the salon on my own was tiresome, but I believed that with determination and progress forward, my beliefs would be acknowledged. Almost weekly, I heard, "Corrine, how do you do this, raising three young children on your own?" The answer back was always the same: "I believe in hard work and anything is possible." The hours of work and frustrations of failure made me smile because I knew my potential was being released.

Unfortunately, the dream was put on hold. The finances were not enough to keep the vision going and the area I chose to put a salon in was in the wrong part of the city. The area was hidden from mainstream traffic and only one other business occupied the street. The building was over one hundred years old and had a Victorian architecture vibe, high ceilings, and fragrant oak floors. The interior design creativity that I created was a mere masterpiece on a minimal budget. This wasn't the end of the vision as I still held on to the belief in working hard and not stopping; looking back was not an option.

This was when the visuals of my inner force took me to the next step. I ignored the advice of numerous family members and friends when I decided to leave a corporate job and become fully self-employed. "Corrine, you have a great paying job. Why would you move and uproot your family?" My answer was defined and concise. "Because I have a clear vision of what our life will look like, and I will work hard to bring it to reality." Beliefs give us the drive to open the door to numerous potentials when combined with a clear vision.

One thing I was very good at was visualizing outcomes both for myself and others. I didn't always use this gift to my full advantage. Hearing family and friends call me crazy was the spark that set my dreams and visualizations into high gear. I always stayed strong in my vision of a pet grooming salon with a retro vibe unique to all the others.

My kids and I packed up most of our belongings and headed off on the next adventure. The larger city seemed a place where I could impact the world and have more opportunities for my children to thrive. For some reason, this move made me feel calm.

I would visualize both on paper with wild drawings of layouts and themes. The main visions were in my conscious mind and collectively held together with my belief system. This sounds like I had it all together, but I struggled with self-doubt and fear. The only thing I had a strong hold on was keeping this vision alive in my mind. Visualizing my success and thriving through difficult times enabled me to kickstart my life as an entrepreneur, allowing me to access the deeper aspects of my potential.

I can remember the inner struggle that kept playing out in my mind. It was like a marionette puppet show. I was being led in different directions and it felt like societal pressure was pulling me in the direction I did not want to go. A former partner once retorted, "Corrine, you need to get back to reality!" This negative response ignited more of my inner passion. I moved forward with an unleashed power I had not had before to uncover my hidden magical potential. I decided that my journey was without this person and I continued to create my vision.

Some people say the grander your vision, the crazier you are. I believe this makes outstanding entrepreneurs. Onwards and upwards! After many creative drawings and sleepless nights, my vision was coming true. After pushing through all the struggles with ego and outside influences, I found my power, and magic started to happen. Lack of vision can hamper your desire to tap into your hidden potential. Having a vision—some call it a dream—gives you something to look forward to and create.

It is said that when you visualize your dream and have a strong belief system, manifesting becomes a superpower. I was visualizing a second pet salon and holding strong to my beliefs. Raising my three children alone and living off a line of credit with only $3,000 left to spend, I decided to take the risk and went for it. The world began to create synchronicities and people came out of the woodwork to help me achieve this dream. Plumbers, carpenters, and business mentors bartered for pet grooming services. Many nights I would ask, "Why are these people helping me?"

For the answer to that question, I would have to stop and think back to cancer, domestic violence, and tragic accident. I used these past hardships to ignite and dig deep into my source of inner potential. This is often the case when we get backed into a corner and our only way out is moving forward. I had a purpose to bring this pet grooming vision alive. I put my best foot forward and the salon magically began to come alive on another extremely low budget, and many angels came to help me achieve the dream.

My creative visual prowess was cultivating an inner space beyond the norm for local salons. The salon was finally completed, and when business began, it was euphoric. Business began to blossom and I had enough money to pay my rent. Unfortunately, devastating news came my way. The landlord had not zoned the property and the city shut me down with fifteen days' notice to vacate. After this notification, I was crushed and cried many nights alone. I looked at my three sleeping kids, wondering if we were going to be homeless, and it brought me into another reality. I had to once again dig inside my inner power to pull out another handful of potential.

I frantically had to start visualizing alternate routes and working corporate was not one of them. Then another miracle happened and the by-law officer that shut me down helped me find a temporary location up the street. It was just a room where I could sustain my clientele, but it created income to survive. I had customers console me and one business mentor told me, "Corrine, don't give up, you are different and incredible." This angel and others helped me to believe in myself and keep my inner potential flowing. Every failure in my life has led me to another vision that would dig deeper into my magical potential that otherwise would have been untapped. This was another creative vision that led me to my next venture in the pet grooming industry. This time I completely combined my beliefs and visions, but more importantly, I sought to think outside the realms of the basics. It was another key to unlocking the magic.

The final step in unlocking my potential in this journey of entrepreneurship would be different. I always loved my little mischievous grin when I expressed my visions to people who were not of the same mindset. I sometimes savored watching the reactions of people on the other side of my creations.

The way I delivered my creative process in all the salons was with the flair of my personality and cutting-edge branding. The customers these salons attracted were people who had the same mindset. The exploration of unique strategies and implementing creativity on an extremely minimal budget was something that astounds me to this day. Innovation and exploring alternate ways of doing business create an avenue for you to show your inner potential and authenticity.

Losing my first salon in the big city and relocating to a smaller space up the road enabled me to push forward toward even bigger dreams. This time I planned to go beyond the other salons and use the unfortunate events as a catalyst. I intertwined my beliefs with unique visualizations. I remembered past events that pushed me to move through the fear of failing again.

"Corrine, you have cancer and will likely live one more year."

"Corrine, you will have to live in the domestic violence shelter for six months with your three kids."

"Corrine, you will have to undergo facial surgery to repair the damage to your nose."

As counterintuitive as these statements may appear, they were critical for me to fulfill my highest potential. These events also fueled my drive to live in the moment and be grateful for every blessing. The next salon was a true exploration of my need to express and live outside the circles of the ordinary while delving into the whirlpool energy of my remaining potential.

With sheer determination, I found another location for the next pet salon. I had paid down enough on my line of credit to pay the rent and deposit. The space was 700 square feet and in a plaza. With a place secured, I began to create and plan the vibrant salon that was inside my head.

I was trying to meet people in the big city when a synchronicity happened. I met a fella that seemed to appear out of nowhere, and we hit it off immediately. It was more like a friendship than an intimate relationship. We'll call him Rick, and he was an angel who came to me to help me with the renovations of the salon. This friend happened to be a carpenter by trade and offered all his services to me for free. I just had to bring him dinner when he was working late in the salon.

What a blessing that this happened to me! As I was a little in over my head with the extensive nature of the renovations. Rick followed my design, and it turned out even better than I imagined. The building of a counter for the dogs to be attached to without cages came alive. This retro innovation was commonly used in pet grooming salons in the 1950s. For some reason, he saw my out-of-the-box vision and believed in my potential. This stranger coming forward was another catalyst for me to believe in my ideas, vision, and nonconformity. Having a belief in yourself can be realized by our hidden power or by the beautiful energy of others.

After two months of long working nights, the salon was up and running. I was beyond happy to see how receptive and engaged the clients were with the eccentric design. It was a success and once the salon was running Rick felt the need to disappear.

“Corrine, it is time for me to move on,” he said in a low, deep voice.

I was devastated. He had become the kind of friend I had not had for so many years. I'm sure he was an angel that came into my life to help ignite my inner potential. We can have all the characteristics to put our potential on fire, but sometimes it takes people outside of us to ignite it within.

The salon grew into a raging success, and I am sure all the angels that appeared came to expose my raw inner potential. I had survived and grown this business to six figures, something I never thought possible. I succeeded in pulling off an exploration of moving outside the normalcy of grooming salons. My potential appeared around every corner, and a drive to succeed was foremost for the next seven years. The roaring success faced another downturn. The place I was leasing was sold and the new owners made changes to the lease, including doubling the rent. I was unwilling to negotiate, as the terms were unaffordable and unreasonable. This is when my innovation to explore and think in a different mindset brought me to start up a mobile dog grooming salon.

I purchased a huge van from the USA and moved all my clients to the new venture. This was the continuation of my beliefs, visions, and exploration out of the norm. The process of importing the van to

Canada was a huge learning curve. However, it was the most amazing finale to opening up my hidden potential as I finally realized all my supporters and angels always saw it. It was like a breakthrough and an awakening combined. I would sit by the ocean in my pet grooming rig and just take deep breaths thinking how grateful I was to get this far. Being able to do my trade and take breaks by the ocean was breathtaking. I also created freedom, which has long been my vision from my mischievous naive girl days. I perceived this as coming full circle, from having many disadvantages in life to having it all.

As I was sitting by the ocean and tears falling down my face, I heard a knock on the window. It was an older lady. She said, "I just had to come and talk with you." I listened to this lady and I couldn't believe that she was a nomad at 85 years old. I was blessed with so much wisdom and knew I was on the right path. She told me, "I was an actor in the movie *NomadLand*." This was truly another angelic moment for my final progression in my career and a sign that I was on the path to becoming free.

From humble beginnings to successful entrepreneurship, my hidden potential was released by my vision, beliefs, and a desire to be different. Through turbulent relationships, cancer, unfortunate accidents, and being a single mom, I strived to hold onto my potential. These events ironically were the catalyst to bring back my beliefs, create my visions, and celebrate my creativity.

The flamboyant flair and daydreaming qualities were other catalysts to bring the unique and eccentric visions alive releasing a mound of hidden potential. Not thinking about the opinions of the world or closed people, I continued to realize these dreams. It wouldn't be complete without being an adventurous and exploring entrepreneur. Combining beliefs and visions became a recipe for being different. Daydreaming in our younger years is our potential just waiting to explode. Sometimes this gets hampered due to generational trauma, but we can always find a way to release it by becoming aware of our inner power.

Watch for all the signs and angels that come forward to support and believe; these people help us dig into our hidden potential. Looking back on this spiritual journey, we don't need all of these characteristics, but just a desire to use our failures and know that we deserve to unlock the hidden potential we had all along.

I hope this story has inspired and filled your heart with hope to unlock your hidden magical potential.

“Unlocking your potential begins with believing that you are worthy of greatness.”

~ Anonymous

CHAPTER SIX

Beyond the Surface: Discovering Your True Capabilities

By Patrick Richard Garcia

When I was first introduced to the concept of "Unlock Your Hidden Potential," many incidents came to mind. In summary, I define it as the sole inspiration to embrace what your present self will do to obtain the best version of yourself. It must feel natural without second-guessing. Including myself, a vast majority of us desire to reach our best potential, as is humanly possible. Not everyone wants to be extraordinary; some are content with their lives, which is perfectly normal. It was something I couldn't embrace initially because I always wanted everyone to reach their best version of themselves. But I always forget that human nature takes over and it is one's own decision whether to strive for the life they want.

Aligning with and fully understanding one's deeper purpose to discover our hidden potential is such a fulfilling experience; it feels like a holistic part of living in the spiritual and physical worlds simultaneously. That is where personal development comes into play. I learned about this during my grade 9 year of high school in 2006, but never took it seriously and didn't give it much thought until graduating in 2009, the final semester. I realized my destiny was not influenced by my friends' concerns and insecurities but rather by my own decision to move in a direction where I can accelerate more of the growth I need to not be held back. I noticed the drastic changes that occurred when I was uncomfortable, taking any opportunity to grow by placing myself in embarrassing situations, but I took the chance to witness how I developed during the process.

After earning my degree in October 2015 and entering the workforce, job hopping without any sort of governance, I was becoming hopeless and directionless. Being unsatisfied and unhappy, it was a downward spiral thereafter. Not tracking my progress, and following what others were telling me to do, I started not to account for my own life. My health, finances, and well-being were starting to take a hit. It was the result of hiding my own insecurities/potential and the inconsistencies I started to build. I was becoming complacent, and I had no one to keep me accountable but myself. It all stemmed from the fears I had that accumulated when I was a child, and I didn't know how to manage it well.

All this deprived me of my ability to still be within my own capabilities and not be able to expand my horizons. One big part of not reaching the kind of individual I desire to be is that the alignment and essence were close to non-existent or not present at all. I was losing my sense of worth and going back to the subconscious thinking that made me smaller than I was. I understood that this work needs to be maintained and sustained consistently due to learning that human nature is something I cannot have control over. Being driven to succeed and honing that purpose requires constant exposure to it. Now, I can speak on how I found my true purpose, identified my calling, and exploited my full potential immediately.

Discovering My Full Potential

Originally, I thought telling my life story was going to be my sole purpose and calling. Being diagnosed with a learning disability at age five forever changed my trajectory. Through every challenge, obstacle, win, loss, heartbreak, and disappointment, I still prevailed—unlike many other individuals who have an LD but never had the opportunity to explore their potential. I knew I had to make a difference and influence other people to be inspired to accomplish, at best, a fraction of the success I had. Because then I can continue to achieve higher and be a public figure out there for people who are misrepresented in my community. However, I discovered that telling my story wasn't enough. I wanted to do more than just share my story and leave it at that.

When I followed extremely successful people with high net worth, who created foundations to give back to the causes they truly care about, it made me wonder what cause I cared about. Public speaking allowed me to share my story, but it needed to find the deeper meaning behind it. I grew up facing many difficulties, with almost no money throughout my childhood until I graduated from high school. I had to save my allowance whenever my parents gave me any kind of money and I had to maximize it. Even with my first job during freshman year at university, I knew the money was going toward my tuition, and I had barely any savings. It was tough. My focus was scattered. I was distracted by other commitments and projects, which included being a chief executive officer for my

Filipino student group and running my own spoken word student group called Poetic Exchange with five student executives.

I always remember my parents' endless sacrifices to give me (and my younger brother) the chance to succeed at something better than my parents had. It becomes a strong motivator to continue doing those actions when tough times and challenges come along. I discovered during the process of growing up that I had an innate ability to connect with people more deeply and could bring them together. At the time, I couldn't understand why or how I had received such a gift, but it became apparent that I needed to use this talent. It wasn't an outstanding one like the ones we always see on live media and television: movie stars, athletes, big-name entrepreneurs, and other influencers. However, once I had identified it, I knew I'd need to put in a lot of effort and compromise to really hone and utilize my talent. Quite often, the things that will take you to your unlimited potential are the gifts that come to you naturally.

Personal Development and Its Challenges

The amount of personal development becomes a mountain to climb when there isn't a game plan developed to apply and execute it. It makes it more difficult when other individuals are not doing similar aspects of it, witnessing the stagnation of people close to your circle. That is something that is out of my control, as mentioned in the beginning—humans have free will to use. Having the kindness to recognize that was initially my weakness—really caring way too much about what could have been the best situation. I also understood that I had no authority or power to do such work, and I felt the compelling role to be an influencer and public figure to influence individuals to do the right thing. The right thing is always to be giving no matter the circumstances one is in. Waiting too long to be successful and be ready is the biggest lost opportunity for developing that impact. All it takes is starting small and increasing it from time to time as determined by your success.

My challenge with philanthropy and combining it with personal development is that self-sabotage is heavily involved. It is implied that as we grow, the subconscious mind always wants to keep us smaller than we need to be. It is a natural part of human nature because success and being out there on a global scale creates that vulnerability. With the constant worry and potential threats that loom anywhere, it is evident that personal development work needs to be applied daily.

Documenting the work and thoughts will help with that. It was the lifelong aspect of continuously growing that became ingrained in my life now that my self-awareness is on an extremely higher level than it was a decade ago. A decade ago, it was not at its peak because I was taking the wrong actions to get there. Not having the mentorship or coaching and not opening myself to different perspectives drastically increased the amount of time and mistakes to reverse the aftereffects of complacency. I found it hard to reach my full potential. Hence, mastering personal development is a Must for every individual who takes on a vision bigger than themselves.

There will always be setbacks, but importantly, watch for the kinds of people that try to bring you back to their magnitude and lifestyle. I have to admit, I still live in my parents' home due to the situation that I am in—living in this city, facing the consequences to equalize my life and rebuilding, and being recently married as well. This situation has created a hurdle for me to work around, kickstarting my momentum. I realized I needed to prioritize the future and temporarily have the middle ground to say that I could manage for two years and be financially ready while developing a whole new mentality to tackle it head-on. Moreover, the friends I have now will propel me to continue reaching my fullest potential. I can rely on my friends when I need a different perspective and opinion and share my wins and losses. It negates all the negativity when there is a strong support system in place to contribute to retaining my desire to unleash my hidden potential.

Types of Philanthropy and the Vision for It

When figuring this out, I recall many causes I was drawn to, such as helping children in third-world countries, solving homelessness, building water wells, building brand new schools, giving unfortunate families funds to assist with their daily expenses, fighting climate change, and so much more. With a large number of choices, I couldn't fathom my final decision on what cause to truly be committed to. The seed was planted when I became a learning disability champion for a private organization late last year in 2023, just before the December holiday festivities. It was great timing because it gave me the momentum to be more involved in the field and be one of the contributors to the field that many children need assistance with. In my experience, most families and individuals that were diagnosed with learning disabilities do not have the best financial situation and are subject to the most prejudice. I was compelled to work within that spectrum on an inner level and figure out what kind of support they needed.

I came up with two components of my philanthropy work: creating scholarships under my name as the primary monetary donor and providing educational and leadership services for the underprivileged children in the communities in which I grew up. The idea for scholarships came from my experience trying to applying for them during my years in university; there was a lack of types for which I was eligible to apply. Many required high grades, which I didn't have. However, a good amount of them express interest through a vast array of essays, short videos, and demonstrations of financial need. By creating a scholarship under my name, there is a legacy persona to that, and it also gives other people after me a chance to create one in their names under their merit. Setting a high financial amount may seem discouraging for the next generation to look at. Nevertheless, this is designed for them to be on par or go even higher than what I contributed. This is meant as a standard and not something that feels impossible.

Having this vision for the long term and for future generations will create stronger individuals and families that will be better equipped to handle a majority of the common obstacles they face daily. In addition, it will assist them in handling uncertainties and doubts about the global atrocities that can substantially alter the course of human history. I can foresee this philanthropic strategy lasting a very long time, as long as there are powerful people who buy into my vision and train under me to continue passing on the knowledge and preserving the wealth of the charitable work that is involved. It is truly the power of giving back that is the most fulfilling aspect of exploring your hidden potential.

Impact and Retaining the Spirit of Achieving Your Full Potential

The most difficult challenge after the emotional pact disappears is retaining the same or similar spirit of your potential. There will be relevant reasons not to undergo this calling. They can be misleading, like a distraction toward another call, but they don't move you the way the first one does. Or life gets in the way, and we slip back into autopilot mode and go back to our old routines that bury our potential. Another reason would be not overcoming fear and deciding not to be courageous enough to take on this calling. While these reasons are valid, they must not prevent you from entering that hypnotic state and envisioning what it will be like to accomplish, at best, a good percentage of your potential. This is not something to do half-heartedly. Every commitment requires full attention, energy, inventiveness, and zest.

One of the key components to maintaining this is to be surrounded by individuals who are doing extremely well and are desirably way off your fundamental base of accomplishments. These people can be your mentors, coaches, a trusted confidante, and even your business partner. If you don't have a business partner, it can be anyone that you can rely on and trust without any bias or ill intentions. You can identify these kinds of people based on your core values, your budget, and what you want to execute. To realize your full potential and create an environment to accelerate the process, the hard and soft skills that were obtained throughout the traditional education system need to be revamped.

As I learned within the Canadian system, starting in kindergarten, I feel it is much slower in comparison to the other educational systems in the world. With my learning disability now behind me, I understand how and why individuals with LD feel much slower than their other schoolmates. Through trial and error to find the right learning style and application strategies, anything can be learned quickly with the right tools, mindset, and resources in place. For a reader like you, there should be no limits to what you can learn. In what to master, mimic, model, and multiply, as my first business mentor Brandon M. Dawson would say, it takes a lot of concentration and finding your foundation until the suitable results occur, to repeat all over again until it stops working. When it stops working, it needs to be re-evaluated and you can start the process all over again.

This is how every successful person in any industry succeeds. They follow a process of what works for them and master the correct skillsets, developing a strong base of fundamentals to increase the output of results. It requires all the holistic aspects of physicality, mentality, spirituality, emotionality, and intellect combined as one unit to accomplish finding your potential.

As we conclude this chapter on unlocking your hidden potential, it's essential to reflect on the insights we've explored together. Each one of us possesses the untapped abilities and dreams that often remain dormant due to self-doubt or external limitations. By recognizing and confronting these barriers, we create an opportunity for profound transformation. This journey is not just about discovering new skills but also about embracing who you are at your core and allowing your true self to shine.

The tools, strategies, and my personal revelations discussed are meant to empower you to take actionable steps toward realizing your potential. Cultivating a growth mindset, setting achievable goals, and surrounding yourself with supportive influences all contribute to your personal evolution. Remember, progress may be gradual, but every small step counts. Celebrate your achievements, no matter how minor they may seem, as they lay the foundation for greater success.

Ultimately, unlocking your hidden potential is a lifelong endeavor filled with discovery and resilience. As you continue to push boundaries and challenge yourself, remain open to new experiences and perspectives. Embrace the journey ahead with curiosity and determination, for the most significant rewards often lie beyond our comfort zones. You have the power to shape your destiny—now is the time to step boldly into the life you envision.

"The most powerful weapon on earth is the human soul on fire. Ignite yours and unlock your full potential."

~ Ferdinand Foch

CHAPTER SEVEN

Find and Embrace: Taking the Time to Unlock Your Hidden Potential

By Laura Jean Denman

This chapter is dedicated to my late father, David Channell, on the twenty-fifth anniversary of his passing on January 25, 2000.

It sometimes takes Time for us to truly feel our potential. I recently learned we have a built-in human compass with an inner guide. If we stand still, listen to, and feel our bodies, the compass can help navigate us, but only if we allow it, and act and remain open.

To tap into this inner compass, we often must step out of our comfort zones and embrace the uncomfortable and unknown.

I've recently been studying the six human needs and found that my top attributes are contribution, feeling love, and connection, which didn't surprise me. I've been involved in the personal development world for years now and had the privilege of working alongside my favorite author, coach, and speaker, Tony Robbins.

In my yoga practice, I've learned about the mythological figure Ganesha. Depicted as a short, stout man with an elephant's head, Ganesha is a powerful symbol in Hinduism and Buddhism. He represents the destroyer of obstacles and demons and is widely worshiped to bring good fortune.

I mention Ganesha because, just like his symbolic role of destroying obstacles, I've learned that only by facing and overcoming my own demons could I finally rise above the barriers that kept me hidden. It wasn't luck, good fortune, or an external force that rescued me—it was the beliefs I attached to myself.

I am a strong believer in finding my spiritual path in this earthly experience. You may relate to the battles and obstacles that have hindered you from discovering or unlocking your hidden potential.

The Beginning

The first step to moving forward in your life is to step out of your way. To do this, you need to spend time with yourself and your thoughts. Beyond the overactive mind, you can reach a quiet, steady place that I like to call awareness. It's in this space that you can ask yourself:

What do I want?

What do I need right now?

What must I become to unlock my hidden potential and be the best version of myself?

Living in Britain, I often hear the saying that we are just too British to ask questions. But that's not me; I was always that curious child at school who wasn't afraid to ask. Years later, I stumbled across an old school report and found a response from my dad to my teacher. It read, "In this day and age, whoever shouts the loudest gets the cake. Laura is inquisitive, knows what she wants, and often goes after it with ambition."

My extroversion, stubbornness, and drive, along with the energy I carry, are qualities I like to consider my superpower and are the keys for me to access my highest potential.

Isn't it great to have such confidence? However, I can assure you that when those moments fade, self-doubt starts to creep in and can be one of the hardest obstacles to overcome.

We all experience moments when we need some extra support. It's crucial to have a cheerleader by your side, someone who believes in you. I'm grateful to my dad and continue to seek others who lift me up. I call this my tribe, my circle, and they know exactly who they are.

I found the quote below three years ago and keep it on my phone as a reminder. I expose my mind to this kind of inspiration frequently to influence my thoughts and perspective.

If you do not go after what you want,
you will never have it.
If you do not ask the question, it will always be no.
If you do not step forward, you will always
be in the same place.
—Nora Roberts

When I reflect on what used to prevent me from using these three steps, the issue often came down to a lack of belief in myself or a fear of failing. As I will share shortly, I essentially lived in fear for a long time instead of being open to possibilities and trusting the process.

We often focus more on what we don't want in life, spending time steering ourselves away from it rather than embracing an open, "anything is possible" attitude. Stepping into the unknown is brave and involves taking chances, as well as asking countless questions along the way.

In my journey of inner work, I've followed the advice to always set my standards higher than I believe I am worthy of. Whether in personal relationships, friendships, or work, it's a continuous pursuit. The goal is to be a little better, braver, or happier each day. But one key lesson I've learned is that letting things flow and trusting the process is far easier than constantly chasing the expectations you set for yourself.

There's always something to chase, but it's important not to get too caught up in that pursuit. Instead, appreciate the time it takes to grow, and unlock new potential along the way.

In this chapter, I will often speak of time. If we rush through challenges, we might miss the beautiful lessons hidden within them. Every obstacle carries a lesson, and it's important to take the time to learn from each one.

How powerful it feels to truly find yourself—embracing both your strength and imperfections, trusting in who you are, and claiming your full potential.

Then Time Stood Still

My story begins on the evening of the millennium. I remember my dad driving me and my girlfriends to our town's dingy nightclub. It was a fantastic night, filled with underage drinking, shenanigans, and the excitement of new hopes, goals, and wishes for the year 2000.

Little did I know that, just twenty-five days later, the innocence of a carefree life would be shattered. At seventeen, life became all too real. Time stopped, and grief overwhelmed my entire being. My world suddenly felt empty and confusing, leaving me adrift in the pain of it all.

On January 25, 2000, my dad went to work and passed away suddenly from a heart attack. The new millennium, once full of hopes and dreams, had instead crushed the life I knew. Nothing would ever be the same again. This was the moment that I thought would rob me of ever reaching my full potential.

Half my lifetime has passed since then. Now, at forty-two, I can assure you that through all the hurdles, challenges, and raw, turbulent emotions, time doesn't stand still—it keeps moving. It sweeps you off your feet when you least expect it, yet also leaves space for long, deep moments of reflection, which I now call grace.

In my late twenties, I fell into a pattern of self-sabotage. My mind worked tirelessly to keep me from seeing my potential, convincing me that I was no longer the person I once was. The innocence and carefree joy I once knew had vanished, replaced by a life that felt heavy and hard. I battled my grief quietly, carrying it alone.

Time standing still is bittersweet for me. These days, I actively practice and promote the importance of allowing time to breathe in the present moment for all that it is. I call this my meditation or shavasana—a sacred pause at the end of a blissful yoga practice. It's the space in which I find stillness and connection, embracing the calm that follows.

The truth is, back then, in my darkest times, my moments of standing still were nothing like they are now. Instead of a blissful pause, they were moments where time felt stripped away, leaving me standing in an empty shell of numbness—detached, lost, and overwhelmed by grief.

As I stood still, alone in the chapel of rest, I remember looking down at my dad, laying there so peacefully. In stark contrast, my heart raced, pounding through my chest, with my mind once again overflowing with questions.

The feeling of time didn't just stand still: it felt like I was being forced to stop. Countless thoughts of an uncertain future swirled through my mind. A flood of emotions overwhelmed me as I realized that our moments together would be lost forever. Suddenly, the idea of living a life of unlimited possibility didn't matter to me. I just wanted my dad back.

I didn't know where Dad had gone, but I found comfort in reading about life after death, seeking mediums, or dreaming. A sky full of stars reassured me that something bigger and better awaited us all when our time came.

I saw a mindful post that said, "Perhaps they are not stars in the sky, but rather openings where our loved ones shine down to let us know they are happy."

I placed a letter beside Dad; it was all I could do to express my final words. Keeping a journal offers similar relief, allowing thoughts to flow out rather than stay bottled up.

I do not know how long I stood still in that room, but I remember making a promise—to keep living, loving, and shining my light where it was needed. I'm the happy soul who uplifts others with humor, full of cheekiness and energy for life. But what happens when the energy is drained, and you no longer feel like the person you once were?

I tried so hard to be that light and show others their potential, but it would come and go. For years, I buried my deepest emotions, unsure of what to do with them. I didn't want to bring others down, so I kept my head up for as long as I could until it became too heavy to hold.

This led me to countless doctors, seeking a fix with endless tablets and beta blockers to slow my ever-racing heart.

The quick fix never came. The tablets now became my numbness.

Another moment of standing still that propelled me to take massive action occurred several years later, during yoga training. I traveled by train to our local seaside town, the first time away from my young kids. As I waved goodbye to them at the station, I felt a mix of guilt and huge relief as the weight of freedom and responsibility lifted from my shoulders.

I was optimistic that I would learn how to manage my mindfulness. I realized that, for a while, I had felt like a kettle on the boil with a whistle that was in overdrive, rattling in my brain. It was physically and mentally exhausting to keep silent, though, of course, no one else could hear it.

I had heard a podcast by Mel Robbins that said, to be a good parent, you must learn to parent yourself. That became my intention. How else can we help our children reach their full potential if we don't expand into our own?

I had the best time that afternoon, enjoying moments alone on the beach. I couldn't remember the last time I had the opportunity to let time stand still, granting me this headspace and freedom. It felt exhilarating, like I could finally breathe. But later, during training, we were asked to find a partner, stand face to face, and simply stare deeply into each other's eyes in silence.

My partner was beautiful, standing tall with the most amazing eyes and a wonderful smile. This became one of my most heart-wrenching, awkward, and uncomfortable moments. I had to tolerate the stillness and silence, not making a scene, just standing there and watching as time and space unfolded in that moment.

For me, that moment took me right back to when I had to lock my legs stiff to stand while watching the curtain slowly wrap around Dad's coffin as it was lowered into the incinerator. That moment hadn't occurred in silence, though: I had pre-recorded myself singing *My Heart Will Go On.* My dad loved to hear me sing; he was my number one fan. My voice echoed through the packed crematorium, yet you could hear a pin drop in what felt like a long, drawn-out silence. It was so raw and still, and my head urged my body to race over and fight or do something—but to what end? I knew I had to stand there and be brave. Moments like these can drain our will and keep us from living a life of limitless potential if we assign a disempowering story to the emotionally significant events that we all experience. The yoga training was my support to help me create powerful meanings to the events that happened in my life.

This time, I had someone standing about an arm's reach in front of me, gazing into my soul. All I could think about was whether she could see my hurt, my pain, my suffering. I wondered if she could glimpse the ugly, deep, dark place I felt trapped in.

Could she see it or feel it? I felt awful about how that might reflect to her—the shame, the guilt, the pain, the vileness of it all. How could she even know? I thought I could put on a brave face and smile—after all, I was getting pretty good at that. But the intensity of it all was so overpowering, like someone foraging deep in the roots of my soul, inquiring what lies beneath the surface of my being.

Unfortunately, I could not put on a brave front. Tears streamed down my face. I tightly squeezed my eyes shut so she wouldn't have to witness it, but then I had no choice but to excuse myself to the nearest bathroom. I felt like I was going to combust!

Remember that kettle and its whistle? It was at a boiling point again, and I felt on fire everywhere. Inside, my body was hot and sweating, yet I was shaking as if I had just undergone cold immersion therapy. "Great idea," I thought as I splashed cold water all over my face.

I so badly wanted to interact with others on a soul level, seeking compassionate and open honesty. I knew I would get there, but the time wasn't right yet: first, I needed to work inward. If we don't attend to the emotional pain suppressing our potential, how can we live life to the fullest?

This decision to turn inward was the bravest thing I could have done. It takes courage to face your demons and determination to make it happen. It is here when my relationship with yoga and my inner self began—and wow, was this a journey to unlocking possibilities!

During my journey of self-discovery, I've encountered unqualified teachers who, instead of guiding me professionally, attempted to break me emotionally using unsafe methods. Their approach lacked the integrity and care essential for true healing. I cried every day, and though this helped me release buried emotions, the layers of my heart still felt like skin needing to be shed, like that of a snake. I found strength from within, and my stubbornness resurfaced, refusing to let the process defeat me. I passed and qualified as a yoga teacher, then pursued life coaching for children and adults. This is where my heart softened, and I rediscovered love both for myself and more of my potential.

I practiced loving-kindness repeatedly until I felt my light return within me.

I realized that my hidden potential was ready to emerge—my time had come. I planned to help others fall in love with themselves through yoga, a supportive lifestyle and space where people uplift one another and share their trials and triumphs. My mission was to hold space for women, ensuring no one feels unworthy of self-love or joy in life.

Everything seemed to be shaping up: I had a perfectly wonderful husband, three kids, a house, a close childhood best friend, and a mother, both of whom were like soul mates, cheering me on. Yet, I still felt lonely, craving connections with more like-minded people who shared my passions. That's when I decided to set up my business and the idea of building a women's circle.

Looking back, how could I have everything yet feel so lonely?

Was it postnatal depression? Who knows—I didn't label it. Maybe it was the fear of failure, as frustration had grown from the feeling that my existence had become stagnant. I had poured my heart and soul into being a mother, dedicating everything to raising happy, healthy babies. I can't stress this enough to all mums: the expectations we place upon ourselves can be overwhelming. Those self-imposed pressures kept pulling me down time and time again. When we aren't seeing progress in our lives, our unlimited potential can seem so far away. It's almost like taking two steps forward and three steps back.

I had also lost close family members and friends who passed away due to illness. Grief is a strange thing that lingers even when you think you've conquered it, resurfacing with every new loss. I was deeply saddened by losing more important people in my life. With that, my anxiety returned, along with health complications: heart palpitations, insomnia, low self-esteem, panic attacks, migraines, and visual disturbances.

Did you know that your body gives you signs when something isn't quite right? The most important part of my story is this: stop, take the time to listen to your body, and then take full, intentional action to repair whatever needs healing. Why? Because optimum health is optimum potential.

It took years, but with pure determination and no medication, I made progress. I joined a Buddhist community, started a yoga practice, read self-help books, and discovered my personal development leader, Tony Robbins. I signed up for courses in life coaching and mindfulness and embraced a healthier lifestyle.

You see, it's all about taking time to heal, time to feel, time to process, time to breathe, and time to acknowledge. We must accept and honor that we are humans on this planet, here to live and experience life. Ultimately, that life is ours to shape.

Tips I Learned to Support Your Potential:

1. Listen to your body: Pay attention to the signs your body gives you. If something feels off, take the time to investigate and address it. A healthy you is your highest potential.

2. Practice gratitude: Make it a habit to recognize and appreciate at least one good thing in your life each day.

3. Embrace self-care: Prioritize your mental and physical well-being. Engage in activities that nourish your body and soul, such as yoga or meditation.

4. Surround yourself with support: Connect with like-minded individuals who uplift and inspire you. Community is vital for growth.

5. Seek knowledge: Invest in your personal development through books, courses, and mentorship. Learning from others can provide valuable insights.

6. Allow yourself to feel: Embrace all your emotions, both positive and negative. Acknowledging your feelings is a crucial step in the healing process.

7. Take action: Once you recognize what needs to change, take proactive steps to implement those changes in your life.

8. Be kind to yourself: Recognize that healing and growth are ongoing processes. Be patient with yourself as you navigate your journey.

9. Cultivate mindfulness: Practice being present in the moment. This helps reduce anxiety and increases your appreciation for life.

10. Celebrate your progress: Acknowledge the steps you've taken, no matter how small. Every bit of progress is worth celebrating. When you focus on your potential, it expands and grows.

11. Always lead with love: Love is an example to follow. People feel it is a ripple effect that enables you to find joy and the moments that make your heart sing. This is one of the unlimited ways of unlocking your hidden potential.

In yoga, we call this living in your Dharma. Living your purpose, your calling in life.

Living your purpose will unlock your potential, creating a snowball effect. Roll with it. Let life throw you curveballs from time to time, and be strong enough to reflect on them. Do the deep inner work when necessary and sit in discomfort. But when the world looks bright, be ready to revel in delight. Take it all in and express your gratitude. Make daily meditation a part of your routine and start a practice that feels good in your body.

Embodied movement provides the energy flow you need to step confidently into the world.

The physiology of the body strongly influences how you move forward. Be bold, stand tall, and be a giant among the crowd. Yes, even at five feet, four inches, I don’t need height to measure up to my higher self—just a little bit of self-belief. If it takes a little bit of time for you to find your self-belief, then borrow someone else’s. Seek out a positive mentor or coach and surround yourself with good company.

How you choose to do things becomes a pattern and habit within your entire framework. You decide when to turn your light on; no one else can make that move for you. The hardest part is overcoming the overthinking and the expectations we place on ourselves.

Remember that time is a gift; don't waste your hidden potential on unfilled dreams.

What is life if it is never lived?
What is love if you have never loved?
What is pain if you have never felt it?
What is inspiration if you have never been inspired?
What is transformation if you have always remained the same?
What is worth if you never feel worthy?
What is courage if you never take a leap of faith?
What is the answer if you never ask the question?

I encourage you to find peace and an understanding of who you are. Make time to stand still for yourself, then lean into the unknown and explore all of life's obstacles and opportunities with grace.

Many things can change—the good, the bad, the ugly—and the synchronicities that occur are often beyond our control or understanding. We may never know why things happen to us, but we can choose to embrace the journey. We can let our story be a catalyst as we fall in love with the rhythm and vision of life.

"To unlock your full potential, you must first unlock your mind and expand your belief in yourself."

~ Anonymous

CHAPTER EIGHT

My Cosmic Leap: Illuminating and Outlining the Invisible Nexus Within

By Lynn Hayward

The screen went blank, and, for a moment, so did my mind. But in that digital void, a universe of possibility exploded into being—my personal, unexpected big bang, switching on the infinite ignition to create my nexus spark! What I thought was a glitch in a Zoom call turned out to be the birth of a nebula of potential within me.

I found myself drawn into a profound stillness, and in that stillness, it was as if the cosmos had paused with me, as if all that existed was the quiet vastness between stars, inviting me to listen. The darkness wasn't emptiness but an entryway—a threshold where all possibilities converge and illuminate. It was in that split second of darkness that the entire cosmos seemed to speak, not with words but with an undeniable force. In that silence, something greater stirred, and from the void came the question.

At that moment, the blank screen became more than a technical error; it became a microscope, revealing hidden galaxies of possibility within me. This darkness, like dark matter, was shaping the unseen architecture of my own universe, offering a reminder that what feels like an end can often be the beginning of something infinitely vast.

I saw time and creativity as precious interstellar currencies, shaping the unseen structure of our personal universes like dark matter. The blank screen became a microscope, a focal point, revealing vast, unexplored galaxies of possibility within me and very likely in each of us… If that is our desire.

What I didn't know then was that the darkness held the seeds of something far greater. From the silence, a universe was detonating, and I was starting to hear it—a cosmic invitation, quiet at first, then louder.

This unexpected moment of digital darkness illuminated a profound truth: every perceived failure is a cosmic invitation to explore hidden dimensions within. This moment of darkness was my event horizon—a point of no return, reshaping, outlining, and illuminating how I saw myself and the world forever. In the quiet, I felt it—the gravitational pull of possibility, as if the universe itself was calling, asking.

Each of us faces moments when the world seems to pause, offering us a gateway to vast inner landscapes and a journey of self-discovery. In that silence, each challenge holds the spark of new galaxies within. Unlimited potential.

As I stared into the dark screen, I understood I was not alone. The cosmos within me was a mirror of the boundless universe around us, each of us a galaxy woven together by threads of shared experience, potential, and dreams.

Standing at the edge of understanding, I felt the pull—not just of the universe beyond, but of my inner cosmos. The darkness asked a silent question, marking a point of no return.

This journey of self is not just a personal exploration; it's a cosmic journey through an ever-expanding universe of possibility. Together, let's uncover how each moment, each challenge, is a gravitational force guiding us towards our brilliance.

The universe is our grand canvas, encompassing all that exists, extending beyond all we can see. As we venture into our potential, we are not just spectators but co-creators, actively painting our lives on the infinite canvas of existence.

A Contract with Oneself – Setting Intention as a Cosmic Map

As I stared at the #blankblackscreen, a shift took hold within me, like a new constellation forming in the depths of space. The depth of value started to morph in my imagination.

At first, the screen seemed empty—a matte black canvas, vast and unadorned. But as I looked closer, it was as if the void was alive, pulsing with hidden stars, planets, nebulae—a cosmos of potential waiting to be seen. At that moment, I turned my gaze inward and found this same cosmic landscape mirrored within myself. #Athoughtnebula swirling in distant personal constellations, burning like an emotional supernova, all connected by an invisible thread of experience. Each thought, feeling, intention, and promise emerged as a glimmer in the darkness, a guiding light on the map of my inner universe.

This contract with myself is more than a list of goals; it is a sacred constellation, a map of vows that guides me when the path blurs. Each intention I set is a point of light, a star in my inner sky, anchoring me to my purpose. These promises are my North Stars, illuminating the boundless landscapes of potential. In the stillness between breaths, I listen to the whispers of my soul, crafting intentions that are not mere words—they are stars I can navigate back to, no matter how far I roam.

When I vow to embrace creativity, I'm not just making art; I'm channeling the dynamic energy of creation, translating the invisible into form. Each act of innovation is an offering, a light I add to the cosmos. When I choose compassion, I open my heart, recognizing that we all share this vast, interconnected constellation. Every promise becomes a guiding star, reminding me of who I am becoming, even amid shadows and doubt.

This celestial contract is a living map, a pattern that evolves as I do. Just as the night sky shifts with each season, my intentions transform, reflecting my deepening understanding. I adjust, refine, and sometimes let old stars fade to make space for new ones. My time, energy, and creativity are the stardust from which I shape my reality, invested with intention and care. These vows become the currency that propels my journey, turning each step into a pathway of growth and resilience.

Cosmic rivers connect different aspects of my being, sometimes calm and steady, other times turbulent, destructive, and transformative. I see experiences as the planets orbiting the central star of consciousness, each one shaping my personal universe in its own unique way.

I believe in my magic—my inner cosmos is woven with invisible threads into a vast constellation of shared experiences, dreams, and emotions. Each of us contributes to an ever-evolving universe of human potential. When I grow, I am not only expanding my universe; I'm part of the collective expansion of our cosmic consciousness.

Moments of transformation—my inner supernovas—send ripples through this shared fabric, igniting potential in others. Just as a dying star seeds new worlds, my breakthroughs spark light in the lives around me. We are all interconnected in this cosmic dance, constantly expanding, influencing, and inspiring each other.

Every insight I gain is a spark in the darkness, a ripple in the universal web that touches others. None of us is alone in this process; we are galaxies in motion, pulled together by shared growth. Our combined energy—the supernovas of our emotion, creativity, and insight—stretches the boundaries of what's possible, connecting us all in an endless cycle of expansion.

This interconnectedness is more than poetry; it's the essence of existence. Every action, every story, every creation sends ripples through the cosmic web we share. My self-discovery is bound to the journeys of others. As I unlock my potential, I help others unlock theirs. Together, we rise.

Creativity as Cosmic Alchemy – Transforming Pain into Art

Creativity, my interstellar process that transforms life's rawness into beauty and meaning. Through every brushstroke, word, or pattern, I transmute fragments of light and shadow, joy and sorrow, into a constellation of insight. Each creation is a luminous expression of my journey and a bridge connecting me to universal truths.

In this process, I am both the artist and the art, turning pain into inspiration and joy into light. My creations transcend self-expression; they become gifts, points of connection in the shared tapestry of human experience. Just as stars shine brighter together, my art resonates as part of a collective truth and resilience.

Tools like storytelling, art therapy, self-awareness, and introspection form my palette. Storytelling weaves meaning into my experiences, while art speaks the inexpressible. Self-awareness serves as my compass, guiding each act of creation—a cosmic dance that transforms my inner world into something others can see, feel, and connect to.

As an alchemist, I embrace the rawness of life, turning challenges into catalysts for transformation. Difficult emotions are not burdens; they are the *Prima Materia*, the primary substance from which wisdom and growth are forged. Obstacles are not blockages; they are sparks of potential.

The alchemical process begins with **awareness**—facing both light and shadow without flinching. This awareness acts as the crucible, focusing the energies needed for transformation. Next comes **acceptance**, not as resignation, but as fuel—an alchemical fire that powers change. **Intention** follows, shaping the path of transformation, and the **action** turns intention into reality, like the alchemist's steps in creating gold.

Patience and persistence are essential in this process. Transformation unfolds in cycles, each one refining me further, revealing layers of value and insight. I draw on tools and resources—books, spiritual practices, the wisdom of others—which are like instruments in the alchemist's lab, enhancing my ability to evolve.

In this cosmic alchemy, I am not alone. As I transform, I become a catalyst for others, my growth sparking ripples of change throughout the cosmic community. Together, we turn our experiences into art, our journeys into stars, and our lives into a shared constellation of potential.

Mindfulness as a Galactic Compass – Navigating Uncertainty

In the vast, unpredictable universe of life, challenges are not roadblocks; they are gravitational forces capable of stretching me to new attitudes. Like a spacecraft gaining momentum from a planet's pull, I can harness obstacles to propel me forward. Each challenge I encounter—whether a difficult decision or a personal conflict—becomes an opportunity to cultivate skills, deepen relationships, and reveal strengths I didn't know I had.

Introspection is my compass on this cosmic journey, my anchor in the swirling uncertainty. With each breath, I connect to the progression of the universe, grounding myself amidst the unknown. Mindfulness doesn't remove challenges, but it helps me approach them with resilience and grace, transforming each moment of doubt into a field of potential.

Through centeredness, I learn to see obstacles not as immovable objects but as cosmic launch pads. Each breath infuses me with calm, reminding me of the vast potential within every moment, no matter how daunting. Obstacles become hidden reservoirs of energy, and when I overcome them, I convert this potential into forward momentum, unlocking new depths of strength and creativity.

Mindfulness teaches me to conserve my energy and direct it with intention rather than scattering it through worry or fear. Every conscious choice is a guiding star in the #landscapeofmylife, helping me outline my path even when the future is unclear. By staying present, I honor my unique measure, embracing both light and shadow as integral parts of my journey.

This practice doesn't just center me; it connects me to the larger universal community. Just as stars cycle through phases of light and darkness, we all navigate the duality of clarity and obscurity, confidence and doubt. Together, our mindful breaths create a constellation of resilience, a shared web of strength that lights the way for us all.

In this attentive space, I let go of what no longer serves me, creating room for new insights and possibilities. Each challenge becomes an intergalactic gift, deepening my understanding and strengthening my bonds with others. Through presence, I don't just survive life's mysteries; I navigate them with curiosity, finding freedom in each moment of presence.

As I journey forward, mindfulness remains my orbit, guiding me through the infinite landscapes of my inner universe. Every breath roots me in humility and purpose, reminding me that life's uncertainties are not barriers but invitations to realize more of my potential. Together, as mindful travelers, we create a constellation of shared strength, each breath adding to the light that guides us through the unknown.

The Universal Linking of Multiple Transformational Currencies:

For me, time is my most valuable and precious currency, a cosmic river that shapes my life. How I spend it defines the course of my personal universe. Am I using it to deepen connections, expand knowledge, and pursue passions? Or am I allowing it to slip into black holes of distraction?

In my cosmic journey, I am guided by currencies of essence, not wealth—forces that shape, transform, and propel me forward through the universe within.

Energy is the fuel that powers my journey, a fire that burns like the core of a star. It's the force that drives me to pursue my goals, to rise above challenges, and to breathe life into my potential. Am I directing this precious energy towards what aligns with my soul's purpose or am I draining it on pursuits that leave me empty?

Creativity is my cosmic alchemy, the power allowing me to envision new worlds and bring them to life. Beyond artistic expression, it is the force of innovation, transformation, and reimagining of what could be. Am I nurturing this gift, or am I letting it be stifled by self-doubt and hesitation?

Visualization is my telescope, a lens to the stars through which I can see beyond the present moment into the potential future awaiting me. Am I using this vision to map paths towards dreams that light me up or am I allowing it to dim under the weight of past disappointments and limiting beliefs?

Skills are the tools I wield on this vast journey. They are not static or finite but evolving capacities, ever-growing and changing, like galaxies in motion. Am I daring to expand these abilities, to learn and refine, or am I clinging to the familiar out of comfort?

Emotions are the colors in my inner cosmos, painting each experience with depth and vibrancy. They guide my perceptions, my choices, and the way I navigate the inner landscapes. Am I embracing my emotions as sacred guides, or am I letting them rule over me, unchecked and unacknowledged?

Empathy is the binding force, the gravitational pull that connects me to others, creating constellations of shared experience. It's the bridge that allows me to feel, to understand, to connect beyond myself. Am I nurturing this bridge, letting empathy flow freely, or am I allowing it to wither in isolation?

These currencies do not exist in separation. They intertwine like cosmic rivers, converging into a powerful current of transformation. By consciously investing in each, I amplify my journey, accelerating my evolution and deepening my well of potential. This dynamic ecosystem within me is alive, expanding with every mindful choice and every intentional action. Through these currencies, I don't just navigate the cosmos—I become a creator within it, shaping my universe with purpose, vision, and boundless potential unearthed.

The 360° Step Forward Nexus of Inspiration and Innovation

As I span the ether of potential, it's important to recognize that inspiration is not a one-time event, but a cyclical process. It's a cosmic rippling of giving, receiving, and seeking that propels us #foreverforward in our journey. As I previously wrote in my last chapter, "Reimagining the Nexus of Art."

"Rooted in my personal ethos of 360 Degrees-Forward, I champion the fluidity of expression and the cageless potential within us all. By embracing the unconventional and nurturing a belief that sharing and caring forge powerful narratives... My commitment is resolute: to design a space..."

No matter which way I AM heading
in my 360° space
I AM always
#facingFORWARD or
#FORWARDfacing
Solutions I seek
are consistently within reach.
It's potential.
My intrinsic mindfulness
and redesigning choices
that determine the quality
of my unique
pay it forward journey.
Surprises emerge
from my
'cocooned' perspectives.
Anywhere, anytime!

I imagine inspiration as a celestial body—a moon moving through phases. In the 'full moon' phase, I am radiant, brimming with ideas and energy, sharing my light freely. It's a moment to become a beacon for others—a flare in the night sky, illuminating paths for those in the shadows.

Then comes the 'new moon' phase, when my vision dims and creativity feels hidden. In these quiet spaces, I turn outward, seeking light from nature, art, and the stories of others. Here, I allow the glow of the world to reignite my spark, allowing external light to fuel my journey back to inspiration.

Between these extremes are the 'waxing' and 'waning' phases—moments of build and release when inspiration grows or fades. These are times to nurture creativity deliberately: to journal, to meditate, to explore new perspectives. I reflect on past sparks, rekindling my passion during these softer phases.

Understanding this cycle of inspiration lets me move gracefully through the ebbs and flows of creativity. When I am low, I know that inspiration will wax full again. When I am overflowing, I channel that energy outward, contributing to the shared pool of inspiration that connects and binds us.

In this rhythm, a beautiful symmetry emerges. Each phase invites me to shift roles—sometimes the giver of light, other times the seeker. This cosmic dance between teacher and student, giver and receiver, deepens my humility and gratitude, reminding me that we are all interconnected, each phase linking us in the grand tapestry of unlimited perspective.

The Cosmic Classroom of Life

As I journey through the universe of my potential, I see life itself as a cosmic classroom, where each experience and interaction is a lesson as varied and abundant as the stars.

In this curriculum, there's the astronomy of self-awareness, where I study my thoughts and emotions; the physics of relationships, teaching me about attraction, repulsion, and balance; and the chemistry of growth, where elements of my personality combine to form something new.

Challenges are not traps—they are exercises to help me apply what I've learned. The difficult conversation? It's a pop quiz on empathy and clear communication. The project that feels beyond me? It's a group assignment in resilience and problem-solving.

Here, there are no failures—only lessons. A setback becomes a study in potential; mistakes are masterclasses in adaptability.

In this cosmic classroom, we're all both students and teachers. My experiences offer valuable lessons for others, just as their perspectives enlighten me. Together, we weave a tapestry of wisdom, each thread adding to our collective understanding.

To truly engage with this cosmic curriculum, I approach each lesson with curiosity, listening with my heart and intuition. Just as an astronaut must leave their spacecraft to explore, I, too, must step beyond my comfort zone to discover new facets of potential.

Learning here isn't about accumulating facts—it's about transformation. It's about evolving into a more aware, compassionate, and empowered version of myself. Each lesson isn't just information; its formation, shaping my character, refining my values, and expanding my capacity to love and understand.

I progress. I see how interconnected these lessons are. Patience learned in one area enhances my relationships; creativity cultivated in hobbies strengthens my problem-solving at work. Each insight ripples through my life, enriching my personal universe.

The Artistic Expression of Self

In the ambitious gallery of expression, I am both the artist and the masterpiece. My life is the canvas, and every choice, experience, and emotion are like digital brushes, adding depth to the composition of my existence.

Consider the vast artistic mediums in this cosmic studio: my words are like poetry, merging emotion into my interactions; my actions, like gravity, are physical expressions of my values; my thoughts, like dark matter, create the measure and shape of my days.

The most profound art is the act of being authentically myself—not a polished image, but a true expression, embracing all my quirks, flaws, and unique beauty. I see myself as a living sculpture, shaped by each experience. Some moments gently mold me, while others feel like meteorites striking. Yet every touch shapes a form that is singularly mine.

Digital art and technology add new dimensions to this gallery. Social media serves as a canvas to express facets of myself; online communities are collaborative spaces where co-creation with others takes place across borders. Virtual realms allow me to step into new dimensions of potential creative expressions.

In this cosmic gallery, my art is alive, breathing, and ever-evolving. Each day invites me to add to my masterpiece, explore new techniques, and experiment with color and form. My self-expression doesn't exist in isolation; it interacts with the artwork of others, contributing to a collective, universal exhibition. My journey of expression has the power to inspire, evoke emotion, and enrich the collective tapestry of humanity.

As I continue to create, I remind myself that there's no 'right' way to make art. My unique style and personal vision is my gift. I embrace the imperfections, the #happyaccidents—where beauty often emerges in the most unexpected ways.

The Celestial Tapestry of Community

As I journey through the universe of my potential, I remind myself that I do not travel alone. I am part of a vast, interconnected cosmic community, each of us a unique thread in the grand tapestry of human experience.

Imagine this cosmic tapestry: each life is a vibrant thread—some running parallel, others intersecting briefly—creating patterns of shared experiences, deep relationships, and fleeting encounters. Every thread matters. The bold threads of leaders catch the eye, but the quieter ones add depth, and even the frayed threads enhance the beauty of the whole.

Our choices, words, and actions ripple through this tapestry, influencing the threads around us. A kind word can make another shine brighter; shared struggles can weave supportive bonds. Creativity can shift the entire pattern, like a comet's tail or a swirling nebula.

This interconnectedness shows me the profound impact I have on others, often in ways I may not realize until much later. It reminds me of the importance of compassion and mindfulness in every interaction, no matter how brief.

During challenging times, when my thread feels tangled, I can draw strength from the surrounding community. The wisdom and support of others help me navigate through dark patches and emerge stronger. This cosmic community extends beyond humanity—it includes all of life, the earth, and the universe. Recognizing this connection fosters a deeper sense of belonging and responsibility, encouraging me to live in harmony with the world.

As I weave my thread through this tapestry, I do so with intention and awareness. I seek to create beauty not just in my life but in the lives of others. Learning from others aids me in expanding my potential. I contribute to a masterpiece far greater than anything I could create alone—the ever-evolving, beautiful tapestry of human experience.

The Ever-Expanding Universe within – Embrace Your Role as Cosmic Architect

As I bring this cosmic narrative of potential to a close, I remind myself that this is not an ending but a new beginning. The universe within me is an ever-expanding, boundless field of potential, inviting me to explore deeper, reach higher, and align more fully with my essence.

I am the architect of my own celestial story, the artist of my life's masterpiece, the alchemist of my own transformation. With the tools of AI, self-awareness, and empathy, I navigate the vast expanse of my inner cosmos, discovering and opening hidden treasures and creating new realms of creativity.

Challenges are not obstacles but cosmic launch pads—gravitational forces that propel me to step forward. #Myinnercurrencies—time, energy, creativity, and empathy—are precious and valuable resources to be invested wisely as I continue redesigning my potential.

I embrace the cyclical nature of inspiration, understanding that sometimes I am the flare and sometimes the astronaut. Each role is essential in the majestic leap of personal and collective advancement. I am part of a cosmic community, a unique stream in the meteor shower of human experience. My self-discovery contributes to a greater whole, a shared trajectory of evolution and linking.

As I step forward, I carry the wisdom of the artist, the curiosity of the explorer, and the alchemist's courage. This explosion of awareness reveals how infinite my "Big Why" must be—to align every thought, action, and ounce of effort with my highest values and boldest dreams. To unlock the vast power within, I synchronize my personal currencies with purpose and precision.

Together, as cosmic architects, we add our unique light to the grand masterpiece, honoring both our journeys and the collective potential that binds us. Let us move forward with open hearts, building a universe that reflects the boundless potential of the human spirit. We are all stars in this ever-growing cosmos, each of us an essential part of the infinite creation we shape together.

Remember: this journey is yours alone; woven into the cosmic society surrounding you. Your story is still unfolding—an endless expansion of potential awaiting discovery. Step forward with courage; the universe within you is calling you to awaken your potential. This is our collective supernova—ever-expanding, always radiating—a cosmic invitation to ignite the galaxies within and reach beyond all limits. Will you answer the clarion call of the cosmos?

Poem: The Clarion Call of the Cosmos

The screen went black
No flicker, no fade—just darkness
In an instant, everything stopped
No warning, no time to grasp or gather
Finished. Caput. End of potential.

But from that blackout
A universe detonated inside me
An explosion of silence turned cosmos
A sudden nebula swirling into life.

I stood at the event horizon
A point of no return
Where gravity pulled not downward
But into the unknown
The darkness asked its silent question
The answer embodied unlimited potential.

In the quiet, something stirred—
A whisper, then a roar
A clarion call from the cosmos itself
Echoing through the void
Will you fall
Or rise to meet the stars?

My thoughts are constellations
Burning bright and bold
Or distant and dim
A nebula of emotions swirling
Cosmic rivers of feeling
Flowing through me.

And so, we expand together
Each insight, a star igniting the dark
Each emotion, a supernova
Shaping the galaxies within and beyond.

From the stars within
We rise—
Not as isolated worlds
But as galaxies intertwined
Ripples in the cosmic sea
Expanding
Unlimited
Potential
Together.

"Our potential is one thing. What we do with it is quite another."

~ Angela Duckworth

CHAPTER NINE

An Open Road of Unlimited Potential

By Darlene Doiron

It was very hectic on the ward that morning; patients were agitated and demanding, and my fellow nurses and I were all over the place, trying our best to deal with everyone. All of a sudden, out of nowhere, a patient grabbed me from behind and put me in a headlock. He was punching me on the side of the head! I felt trapped, scared, and disoriented. I didn't know what to do to get out of his grip; he was so strong! I let out a few screams for help and at the same time tried to fight him off. I felt my glasses fly off my face, my adrenaline just bursting as I tried my best to get away from him!

My coworkers arrived momentarily, prying the patient's grip from my neck and tackling him to the ground. I tumbled against the wall and tried to regain my balance, focus, and assess the situation. Finally getting my wits about me, I realized what had just happened. A coworker picked up my dismantled glasses and my supervisor showed up, putting her arm around me and bringing me to her office. There, she checked me over and asked me what happened. After I told her, she sent me to the hospital for a check-up, and afterward went home to recuperate.

I still remember the pain I felt the next morning after the attack! I could barely move my head; I had pulled muscles and tendons on the left side of my neck. The months following the attack were not easy! I was off work for about six months and in a tremendous amount of pain for a long time, but with medication and physiotherapy, my physical recovery slowly improved. However, during this time, not even once was it mentioned that I should see a therapist to talk about the incident. In my opinion, looking back, attending therapy should be mandatory after any kind of attack. Little did I know that my traumatic experience would lead me to uncover my hidden potential in the most unlikely of ways.

When the time came for me to return to work, I was very anxious about facing my attacker while working in that particular ward. I really did not think I could go back, but I went for a visit on the ward to see how I would feel. Once there, I almost had a panic attack, so I left and asked for a transfer to another part of the hospital where the patients were not as dangerous and unpredictable. Under the circumstances, my transfer was granted.

I was happy to be back at work in another area and with all new patients. The environment was more demanding physically but otherwise much more relaxed. For the next few years, I really enjoyed my job again. I developed a daily routine, but little did I know at the time that I had again become stuck in my comfort zone, doing the same old thing and not growing into my potential.

I was starting to feel exhausted; my sleep was not as good as it used to be. Reflecting on this time, I realize that I was working very hard trying to keep the same level of care for my patients as before. Like everywhere else at the time, there were a lot of cutbacks in our hospital, and our workload was increased. To me, the important people were the patients and they should not have to suffer because of staff cuts. So, I just pushed myself to the breaking point.

I realized I was getting mad at the littlest things, losing my cool with the patients and even my coworkers who did not deserve it. The situation deteriorated to a point where people were scared to talk to me, for they never knew what kind of mental state I was going to be in at that moment. It wasn't fun for anybody. I didn't recognize myself anymore. I started to hate my job and was not happy.

The thought of living into my full potential had never crossed my mind. When I realized I was escalating in a downward spiral, I went to have a chat with my supervisor. I told her how I was feeling and that I was going to go see my doctor and take some time off. She told me she had seen the change in me and was about to talk with me to suggest I take time off. She supported me one hundred percent.

This all happened about five years after I was attacked by that patient. Looking back, I see now that I could have been dealing with a little bit of PTSD. All the reconstruction in the hospital had resulted in us having different patients on our ward; some were more active and mobile, trying to run after you and bite or hit you. You never knew what was going to happen; it was unpredictable. I didn't feel safe, and memories started to flood in of my previous attack. That is when I started to change and my mental health got worse. I realize now that I should have got help a long time before that point.

Once I took some time off, it felt good to be out of the hospital and not have to deal with work or anything else for that matter. I thought I was getting better, but in reality, the tunnel was getting darker and darker every day, to a point where I couldn't see any light at all. I was hitting rock bottom. Not a good feeling at all. There was no living to my true potential at that point!

I did seek help from a psychiatrist and psychologist, but nothing really helped. I was good at hiding how I was feeling when around people, but when I got home, I sure wasn't good. I became depressed and didn't see any way out of the dark fog.

The first thing I knew I had to do was leave town so I could get away and hopefully find a new perspective. I owned my home, but I could no longer afford it and did not want to deal with it anymore. I was going to put it up for sale but had an offer from someone to rent-to-own, so that is what I did. I then moved in with my parents for the time being. I am so grateful for the people who took over my house, and for my parents and friends for always being there for me.

After moving in with my parents, life got a little bit better. I didn't have any responsibilities except taking care of myself and, of course, helping my parents around the house.

At the time, I worked as a ski patrol and had to do one shift a week. This was a chance for me to test my skills and step into my potential, even if I did take the opportunity for granted. I lived an hour away from the ski hill and wanted to keep it up, especially since I had promised my niece that I would take her skiing with me once a week. She was so excited, and even if I didn't feel like going, I could not break my promise to her. I was at a point where I couldn't even afford to put gas in my truck, but my mother would fill it up and make sure I wouldn't have any excuse not to go. It was the only thing I did. She could see how badly I was doing even though I couldn't see it or didn't want to see it. She made sure that I went to work to keep me moving and out of the house.

Well, it didn't take long for the demons to return and take over again. I was feeling so depressed, and all the meds that the doctors had me on did not seem to help. They kept increasing the dosage and adding more to try and find the perfect cocktail! I tried to keep busy during the day, but nighttime was the worst for me. I could not get the voices in my head to shut up. I remember I would play games on the computer after everyone went to bed to try and quiet my mind. Eventually, I would become tired and fall asleep. Sometimes this helped, but not too often.

I still remember that I didn't want to keep living. So many nights, I had my meds lined up on my night table and wanted to take them all so I could end these miserable feelings of emptiness, loneliness, depression, and worthlessness, just to name a few. I felt like I was just taking up space in this world. Even my mom hated leaving me alone for too long because she never knew if I would be alive when she came home. She told me, a few years later, that I never realized how far down I had gone!

Of course, I never followed through with my desire to end it all for one reason and one reason only: my beautiful niece! See, she would come over to my parents' house every morning before school. She would always jump in bed with me to say hi and have a cuddle before she went to school. I couldn't have her find me dead in my bed. I wouldn't do that to her and ruin a young life. She had the innocence of unlimited potential, going about life with such wonder. I am so grateful to have had her be so close at that time.

On my dad's recommendation, I finally found a really good therapist. I was skeptical at first but decided to go see him. I had seen so many people up to now and never got anywhere. After the first visit, I felt comfortable with the therapist; he was a good listener. He gave me exercises to do and techniques to help quiet my mind, which helped me feel better about myself. I had zero self-esteem at that point, and we worked hard together to make me feel better about myself. Self-love was a big part of my recovery and my ability to see more of my potential. I was ready and willing to get better. Trust me, the change did not happen overnight! It took a long time, and I had plenty of setbacks. But my therapist never gave up on me, even when I was giving up on myself. He was used to working with nurses with burnout, and he was good at his job!

After several months of working with my therapist, I was finally seeing a little light at the end of a very long dark tunnel. I kept working hard on myself and was searching for what would make me happy and unlock my full potential. I knew I had a good career but wasn't sure if I wanted to keep working as a nurse or find something else. I had always dreamed of driving eighteen-wheelers and was fascinated by them. But at that time, there weren't too many women in the industry, so that is why I had gone into more of a women-oriented career. Still, the dream was always there; I had put it in the back of my mind for too long.

When I was ready to return to work, I tried going back to the hospital but lasted only three weeks. I didn't fit in anymore, and taking care of patients wasn't what I wanted to do. The routine was too predictable and constrained, and my potential felt stifled. I had enough of that and decided to quit nursing to follow my dream of living into my heart's potential.

I enrolled in a truck driving school near my parents' house. I was the only woman in my class. I thrived in the course; it was the best decision I made. It was finally something for me! I passed my course, finishing second. I was only 0.5 points short of first place! I was so proud of myself for succeeding and finally following my dream.

When you are in such a dark place like I was, you really can't see your full potential! Everything seems so hard and unattainable. After a lot of hard work and determination, I finally unlocked my full potential and followed my dream. What an amazing feeling of accomplishment. Never doubt yourself; no matter how low you get, you still have a lot of potential to succeed!

Within weeks of graduating from my course, I had my first truck driving job and moved to Ontario to start work. Once I finished my on-the-job training, I was finally in my own truck. I still remember the fear and excitement I felt. I was king of the road, and you could not wipe the smile from my face. I was traveling back and forth from Canada to the United States and loved every minute of it.

I was getting pretty homesick, though! The company I was employed by did not travel to the East Coast, which was unfortunate. I applied for a company in New Brunswick, and a friend helped me land the job. Was I ever excited! I moved back home and started my new job. Life was good, and I was so happy. I traveled from coast to coast. My office was the open road, and I had the best view of the world. I had never felt so free in all my life. I did not have anybody to take care of except myself, my truck, and the cargo. I made so many new friends along the way and saw so many places that most people only dream of. Feeling very lucky to have landed my dream job, I felt alive again; I got to see the country and got paid to do it.

Living up to your true and full potential can be challenging. Without a purpose in life, you have no direction on where to go or what to do next. When you find your true purpose and what makes you truly happy in life, that is when you can reach your highest potential. You will always have ups and downs, but the main thing is to never let the downs define who you are. Sometimes, it takes a long time to get back up and see that beautiful light at the end of the tunnel. I am proof that it is possible. It is important to seek help when needed. To me, doing so is not a sign of weakness. On the contrary, it is a sign of strength and willingness to reach your hidden potential.

Go and reach for the stars, and live life to the fullest! You deserve to do what makes you happy. Everything is possible when you unlock your true potential!

"Unlock your true potential by daring to dream beyond what you think is possible."

~ Anonymous

CHAPTER TEN

The Potential Within

By Ewelina Korus

As a child, I felt a strong sense of inner guidance. Nobody instructed me to create vision boards or write down my desires—things most people learn as adults or through courses. I just intuitively did it. This inner compass laid the groundwork for unlocking my hidden potential.

I remember crafting visions in my mind, so many creative views. I still keep some of them, and I'm so grateful that most of them have become a reality. Funnily enough, all I did was write down what I wanted and cross it out once it was achieved. I dreamed a lot about different bathrooms, the most important place in the house to me, and created wonderful designs in my mind. Do you have an important place at home where you feel beyond grateful?

Planting seeds of intention through these childhood dreams—whether it was designing bathrooms, or envisioning diverse futures in hospitality, becoming a marine, or meeting different cultures—was my way of following my inner call. These early practices of visualizing and goal-setting were unconscious steps in a journey to tap into my true self.

In retrospect, I see that every creative thought and dream was a step toward learning to listen to myself, nurturing the seed of potential that lay within. It shows that the journey to uncovering one's potential begins by listening to that inner voice, even when it whispers faintly among the noise of everyday life.

I was always the one in our family eager to explore construction and furniture stores. Alongside that, my love for travel and discovery was ever-present in my daily life. Even during high school, my mind was filled with thoughts of travel, hospitality, and the yearning to live in unfamiliar places. Following this inner guidance, I pursued a degree in Hotel Management and Tourism. While I wasn't initially thrilled about learning languages, this path revealed itself to be a natural fit for me over time.

Our potential is often found in pursuits that spark genuine interest and require no external motivation. Following my heart, I moved to a foreign country. It was a leap driven by my inner voice—a decision that shaped who I am today. Living abroad was a transformational experience that led me to discover so much about myself. It's clear now that taking bold steps and embracing new beginnings are essential to personal growth and unlocking one's true potential.

The five years to get my master's degree weren't easy; there were many moments I wanted to give up, including a desire to move to another country. During this time, logic took over, and I declined the opportunity because I wanted to finish my studies in hospitality and pedagogy, get my driver's license, and follow the logic that this would help me in the future. After graduating, I faced challenges finding a job in my chosen field, due to living in an industrial area. After receiving quite a few rejections, I got a job in hospitality and also a job as a teacher of Marketing in Hospitality.

These vocations were a natural fit for my potential to blossom but I still yearned to live in another country. The whispers to venture beyond my homeland fueled visions of working abroad and experiencing new cultures.

Hearing the strong whispers urging me to move outside my comfort zone inspired me to envision opportunities to move. I saw myself working abroad, learning new cultures, etc.

In my mid-twenties to early thirties, this desire lingered. One warm evening, as my sister enrolled in a driver's license course, she brought exciting news about an opportunity for someone to move abroad for a few months. It was as if the universe was aligning with my dreams, giving me the chance to take the courageous step I had long envisioned.

You can probably guess my answer: I said Yes, Yes, Yes!

I was the one who wanted to go. I knew the job would be below my education level—it was a waitressing position in a restaurant. I remember being terrified on the day of the Skype interview. Having had many job interviews in the past, they no longer felt challenging, but speaking in English was a different story. I knew I had to perform well in the conversation despite primarily using theoretical English during my studies and lacking practical experience.

Fortunately, the interview turned out to be a valuable lesson, and I managed to get through it with my language skills. When you're fully committed to your desires, everything works in your favour. Working at school brought me joy, yet I sensed there was more to explore. Have you ever felt that nagging sense of wanting something beyond your current situation? I never imagined that the lessons of breathing and learning to use my voice would prove so valuable. Stepping out of my comfort zone revealed the incredible power of embracing the unknown. In those moments of discomfort, we often uncover our true potential. This experience taught me the importance of daring to move beyond the familiar. I knew the feeling of building my life in a foreign country would grow, and I couldn't ignore it. Where there is growth, there is potential.

My boyfriend at the time didn’t want me to move; he believed that if I did, we wouldn’t stay together. I was truly in love, sometimes even losing my mind for him, but deep down, I knew there was more on the horizon for me to unlock my potential. The idea of starting something new felt exciting. My mum was against it; she wanted my sister and me to stay close to her. Despite everything, I didn’t let external voices dictate my internal desires.

I’ve always been courageous, though this time I had no idea what awaited me. I said goodbye at the school, and the director even arranged for me to leave earlier than contracted. I was ready to embrace the unknown and head to the Netherlands. I packed my courage, confidence, trust, curiosity for new adventures, a few clothes, a dictionary, a plane ticket, and my excitement for flying—I had never flown before. I took some savings, knowing I might need to work since it wasn’t much, especially when heading into the unknown. At worst, I would have enough savings to return to Poland.

Seeing the beach and the sea was always in my heart, and it was a divine surprise. Everything aligned perfectly. The home of the restaurant owners was a ten-minute walk to the beach and five minutes to the restaurant. I felt immense gratitude beyond words. I discovered so many new things about myself, pushing my flexibility to new limits. I earned good money compared to what I received in Poland. Living with the restaurant owners and eating at the restaurant allowed me to save significantly. Despite missing my boyfriend, I knew my desire was stronger, and everything would become easier with time. The love was strong, but my personal growth was a priority.

Winter was on the horizon, and the Dutch island was closing. The boss asked if I wanted to stay until the next year. I declined, wanting to return to Poland, but promising to return the following year. I spent a couple of weeks in Poland before a neighbor familiar with my experience in the Netherlands offered to help me find a home there, and the rest I did on my own.

Everything aligned with my worth again—a huge new building welcomed me. It had been a great start. Shortly after, I realized the Polish lady I lived with complained about a particular housemate. The atmosphere was strange, but I felt comfortable, as living there felt like home, having the opportunity to cook again, like the Polish tradition of always making a meal at home, which I couldn't do on the island, as the meals had been cooked for me. The Universe listened to my desire and responded. Through this journey, I connected deeply with myself, setting boundaries to allow my soul to feel happy. When your soul and emotions are in harmony, you connect with your true power and can make decisions from a place of authenticity.

Contacts from Texel introduced me by phone to a warm and helpful couple from Bangladesh who I moved in with. They introduced me to wonderful people from a different culture.

We shared meals and I enjoyed their cuisine, though I had to respect their cultural rules, especially regarding guests. They showed me a different way of living that I might never have discovered otherwise. Focusing less on material things, I saw the joy they had, which became the best lesson in practicing gratitude. When you're grateful, you attract incredible things, unlocking hidden potential within.

I met two lovely Polish ladies who became friends, and I often stayed with them for more freedom. I worked in an Amsterdam restaurant and later traveled across the Netherlands to survey Polish people and their experiences. I discovered something essential. The project lasted two years, and during this period, I encountered a bouquet maker through my friends. We worked there briefly, but left soon after, unable to tolerate the poor treatment of people. I knew there was more, and to nurture my soul, I needed to feel free in whatever I pursued. I set my standards high, choosing to work with passion and do what I love. Learning the language and developing myself was critical. Working six days a week and attending an intensive Dutch course was exhausting, but I completed it. However, working in an English-speaking environment didn't improve my Dutch skills.

As spring arrived, I visited Texel as planned, but I also continued enjoying life in Amsterdam. I chose to stay in Amsterdam but went to Texel to inform the owner and say goodbye personally. During this journey, I met a Dutch guy, and we exchanged contact information. Despite initial hesitations, I asked myself whether I should reach out to him. A relationship was the last thing on my mind, but after some doubts, I decided to reach out, leading to a significant learning experience. I tested my intuition, and this was when my unique potential was revealed to me. Testing and learning—even if painful—is crucial for growth. Do you follow your inner guidance during moments of doubt?

I've done this many times, testing my intuition until mastering it. Here's what I do in doubtful moments while making important decisions:

- I distance myself from the decision.
- I take all the time I need to make my choice, ensuring no one and nothing influences me.
- I take a deep breath and meditate to connect with my true self.
- After that, I write the pros and cons on paper.
- I go outside and surround myself with nature.
- I decide to stay true to my purpose.

Despite the challenges, including long commutes and differing lifestyles with my boyfriend, I reflected on my worth and resilience. I nurtured his mind, helping him finish his studies, which was incredibly fulfilling. Learning Dutch seemed never-ending, but I persevered by working in a pizzeria to stay on track. My vision remained clear; I wanted to study interior design, a passion rooted since childhood. Visualizing diverse bathrooms as a kid made perfect sense now.

I stayed focused on my passion despite hardships. My journey highlighted the importance of following my heart, embracing new opportunities, and never losing sight of my personal worth. Every day felt like sitting on packed luggage, frequently overwhelmed with emotion, and I missed my family. The cultural and character differences often saddened me, leaving me tearful before work, yet I kept a smile on my face for customers. However, deep within, I understood this struggle was temporary. This realization unlocked a resilience that compelled me not to give up, knowing in my heart I was destined for more. While I needed a steady income, the work environment felt limiting, exacerbated by inconvenient travel and hours. Despite these barriers, I knew mastering the language was key to accessing my potential, even if it felt like an uphill battle.

Somewhere along the way, I got used to the uncomfortable comfort zone, even facing a lot of pain in these relationships, due to cultural differences and disrespect in some areas of our daily life. I felt disappointed and worn out. When it ended, I realized it had suppressed my potential, constrained my self-expression, and clipped my wings. Instead of lifting me, the relationship constantly dragged me down. When we broke up, I asked myself why I stayed for so long in this relationship and couldn't break off the relationship earlier.

Of course, the consequences meant I had to find a new home quickly. I needed to find something fast—I didn't want to spend more days living together. Speaking with a girlfriend, she mentioned a friend of hers was moving to another country and suggested I speak with the homeowner. After speaking with the owner, I moved into this new room. I was grateful to know the person from my Dutch lessons, who moved to Spain, left the room available for me.

Do you know the feeling when everything seems to go wrong? It was like that. A month after moving, I received news that certain Dutch regulations prevented my work contract from becoming permanent, and the owner requested my return after six months. I had to face this challenge independently. I enrolled in a new Dutch course and engaged in intensive job searching, enduring countless rejections. Although difficult, this process contributed to my development, as writing CVs and cover letters significantly improved my Dutch skills. It was a tough time.

My housemate returned to Italy, and hope flickered within me as I wished for solitude in my space. This wish was granted, and I enjoyed several months alone, finding peace and tranquility; however, persistent rejections took a toll on my confidence. This solitude was pivotal in unlocking my hidden potential, providing the mental space to focus on my goals with clarity and effectiveness. Amidst this, excitement and nervousness mingled as I wondered about the next person who would move in. To my amazement, my soulmate arrived—an unexpected blessing in a time of struggle. This wonderful phase saw me securing a job and transforming our home into a blissful sanctuary akin to a honeymoon. However, life had a different plan, separating us physically, yet our connection remained energetically strong.

This was a time to heal my wounds and raise my vibration to unlock my potential. I wanted to leave this and move to another place, sharing a home with other housemates. It was a short period where I lived with people who didn't serve my potential at all. I looked for my apartment when I felt free and had time to develop myself in all aspects, including nurturing my soul to realize my full potential. The stability at home was crucial.

Though challenging, I knew I deeply hoped to work with my passion. To achieve this, I needed to improve my Dutch significantly. Working irregular hours in-home care made me unsure if it would be enough financially. I used extra time to learn, eventually finding a combination of solutions and workspaces.

My once-strong confidence wavered, and there were countless tears. Although I liked the work, I didn't initially realize its negative impact on my self-worth and happiness.

Seeing joyful clients one day and learning of their passing the next was hard. I fought for better contracts and more hours, growing tired in an environment filled with promises and complaints. They often said, "If you fly with the crows, you get shot with the crows," or "Tell me who your friends are, and I will tell you who you are." Have you ever experienced this? Did you know you need to disconnect yourself from the environment to allow your potential to rise?

I started complaining and feeling unhappy. One of my girlfriends noticed the change, attributing it to my work. While I'd been waiting for external validation, I knew deep down the job was negatively influencing me. Despite earning enough and improving my Dutch, the work environment was toxic. Colleagues would discuss my studies, questioning my worth, as I struggled to find happiness outside my country. It highlighted how some environments seek to dim one's power, which I find unacceptable. Embracing my truth, I remained focused on my goal, seeing this as a temporary phase.

I started clearing my environment, removing a lot of people from my life, and distancing from those who had good intentions for me but didn't want me to open my wings fully. Even for most of those contacts, places I cleaned from my life by myself, Universe helped me a bit—after sending a thought or wish to spend time free without my phone and all obligation of it, two hours later my phone was stolen, and by this way erasing all contacts.

One day, I decided to leave restaurant work behind. I attended an open-door interview for various sectors like customer service, storage, and restaurants in global interior companies. Despite the crowd, I aimed for a customer service role. Days later, I received a call. They had found someone else for the customer service position but asked if I'd use my restaurant experience instead. Though I intended to move away from that, I accepted, knowing the company offered numerous opportunities.

This decision was pivotal, as it demonstrated my willingness to adapt while setting the stage for growth within a big company, eventually uncovering paths that aligned better with my passion.

After three weeks, during my probation period, I reflected and knew I couldn't continue. Recognizing my worth and potential, I spoke honestly with my manager and said I couldn't make it anymore. She valued my work and offered me a position in the bathroom design department. I finally felt aligned with my passion. Although I received an inner voice telling me there was more for me, those thoughts attracted a solution. My contract was not being extended because of the pandemic.

This move was a step toward my passion, showing the importance of aligning work with inner desires. It taught me to trust in the shifts that come unexpectedly but lead to greater alignment with my potential.

These experiences led me to start my own company in Interior Design and Styling. Opening a business is no easy feat, especially amidst Covid restrictions. Passion drove me, but bills were mounting. Confidence in my abilities remained strong, and I knew action was necessary. By daring to start my business, I embraced uncertainty and allowed my intrinsic motivations to drive me toward achieving my potential amidst external challenges.

Balancing freelance work and job applications became my new norm. During an interview for a kitchen design position, I was offered a highly travel-intensive role. I love driving, yet the 220 km one-way commute was impractical, even with hotel arrangements by the owner. Accepting such a role once excited me, but it now interfered with my business-building focus.

In the end, I couldn't make it; the salary was really low, and it wasn't worth putting my shoes on for what I did. It had been challenging but great for personal growth. I knew the pandemic had improved a bit and stayed focused on working on my company, wanting to attract clients to work with me online. A lot of clients didn't want to work online because they weren't sure if I could make it remotely, but I knew I could.

Then the idea came to my mind—hey, let's combine it with some other income streams. Signals had been sent, I guess in the same month I got a call about a stylist position in the bathroom design area—a perfect fit, without even applying for a job. I embraced the role, enjoying the alignment with my passions and past lessons. Even the failure was a lesson for growth. What are you doing while failing, giving up or using it as a power to success?

Embracing this role showed that trusting in my abilities and the Universe's timing could open doors to new opportunities aligned with my passion and lessons learned.

Around the same time, I encountered a coach who introduced me to an online coaching program. This was perfectly aligned with my aspirations, and I enrolled without hesitation. The program asked me to explore my passions, talents, and skills, allowing me to gain a deeper understanding of what I could offer the world. My hidden potential began to awaken.

After facing numerous challenges and setbacks, I reached a turning point in this chapter of my journey. Everything clicked into place as my passions and skills intertwined seamlessly. I immersed myself in coaching, empowering women globally to discover their untapped potential while guiding them to connect with their inner selves and boost their energy levels to visualize their dream lives and take confident, bold steps, which would manifest it. It is such a wonderful feeling see the transformation of other women's lives, and those moments fulfil my own.

Almost as if by magic, this serendipitous flow fulfilled my desire for a harmonious blend of practice and passion, reinforcing the idea that when you're aligned with your true self, the right opportunities naturally present themselves. Sharing experiences and guiding others emphasized how unleashing your potential empowers not only personal growth but also enhances others' journeys to self-discovery and empowerment. I chose to inspire others, focusing on replacing self-doubt with self-belief, weakness with courage, fear with success, and limits with possibilities. Unlocking your potential is about removing self-doubt, boosting energy, and stepping boldly into the unknown with clarity and purpose.

My hidden potential was so overwhelming that I couldn't suppress it any more. I also realized how important all experiences and even lessons are, that those things weren't aligned with my true self and that's why I need to disconnect with it. The desire was so strong that felt if I did not do it, I would die. Of course, it's all experience, lessons learned and token mentorships, while learning different techniques to connect on a deeper level with yourself, boost energy, and effectively visualize during all these years. I have followed various courses and learned from all my mistakes.

I knew there was much more to give to the world from my side, the energy boost I will never forget. Do you ever feel that there is nothing to stop you while having inner whispers to unlock your true potential?

I stopped the coaching program, of course. I took with me what I learned, but I followed again my inner call and got other mentors to unlock my hidden potential, which I did all the time for the past twenty years. Then I started guiding women to replace their limited beliefs with power fuel to discover their true potential and increase their confidence, especially while living in a foreign country. Stay more focused on your goals and have faith, even in heavy moments like facing cancer or just stepping outside your comfort zone. Visualize your dream life!

By unlocking your true potential, removing self-doubts, boosting your energy, and stepping confidently into the unknown, you can visualize your dream life and manifest it with clarity and conviction.

I've learned so many incredible techniques over the years that work so fast into deep connection with myself, increase the level of my energy and visualize effectively with quick results. I love receiving surprises from the Universe, like last time when I sent a thought on December 2022 to the Universe with the wish to move to a newly built apartment. In February 2023, I got the opportunity to make it happen and after about forty days, I started building a new adventure and using my passion for Interior Design as well in the new home aligned with my desire to surround myself with nature.

Thinking of marketing myself with ease, I was invited to write this chapter, thinking of speaking globally. The next day, I got an invitation to be trained by a famous speaker. That's my testimonial of Unlocking my True Potential. What are yours?

When you "Unlock your Potential," the synchronicity is incredibly powerful. As a gift to invest your time in reading my chapter until the end, I will share with you the simplicity that could be useful to unlock your hidden potential:

- Take care of your emotions.
- Be honest with yourself, ask yourself what you want and take actions aligned with your true self.
- Disconnect yourself from people, places, and memories that don't serve you anymore and suppress your unique potential.

Remember, life is a story still being written, and the pen is in your hand.

Seize it.
Embrace it.
Unlock it.

What will be your story of unlocking your hidden potential? What steps will you take to nurture your soul and utilize your potential?

I am open to embracing the beauty of a fresh start with you, letting the pages of your next chapter unfold with the promise of something extraordinary to unlock your hidden potential. Are you ready for it? See you and your life transformation soon.

Additionally, I have whispers in my heart to open doors for virtual and live retreats by 2025/2026. Will I see you there?

"Unlocking your potential means embracing change and having the courage to act."

~ Jack Canfield

CHAPTER ELEVEN

How can trauma be the gateway to your potential? Reflections on Life's Setback Leading into Empowerment

By Annelise Pesa

It felt cold in the oncologist's waiting room. I could see the autumn leaves of October through the algid, aseptic window. The clock marking the never-ending seconds almost seemed to have an angry face.

Everywhere I looked, objects and people beamed hostility or, at the very best, seemed meaningless. I felt like a prisoner just waiting for their sentence of execution.

I confusedly remember the receptionist telling me to sit and wait, the people coming in and out of the clinic, the messages on my phones, and family members calling me. Nothing had the same sense as before the day the doctor said, with a professional yet worried tone, "I'm not too fond of this lump in your breast; you have to check it with a breast specialist."

From that day, my calvary started—first clinging to the hope that it was just a cyst, but contemplating the possibility that it wasn't....and anything could happen.

Will I still be alive in one year?

The story you are about to read is a story of resilience, survival, and developing our potential in the face of adversity.

It is an invitation to reflect that whatever you are going through in this very moment in your life, small or big, if you are still here on this planet, there is hope and potentiality in every situation.

There is still an infinite amount of potential waiting to be born, waiting to be realized. And you will see how the struggle that you are bearing now or bore in the past can be exactly the fire that makes such potential explode!

Developing our potential is found in every situation in which we are thrown in front of chaos, tragedy, or a massive ordeal and realize crudely that we do not have infinite opportunities in life. This realization is a massive catalyst for finding what we want, who we want to be, and what we are authentically good at.

So, going back to my story, what happened then? From there, it was an escalation of oncologist visits, biopsies, appointments, and then the dreaded wait in the oncology room with the angry clock, which brutally kept time to itself. I desperately tried to distract myself from my doomed reality, as a part of my brain was consumed by thoughts like, "This isn't happening to me; it cannot be."

I have always been super healthy and fit—no smoking, no drinking, and yet sometimes things happen to us that are completely outside of our control.

Although for most cancer cases, there is a correlation with lifestyle in a few, there is no explanation. Why did I have to trump statistics and probability? “I am sorry, Annelise, you have [breast] cancer.”

Frozen in shock, I had never experienced this physical sensation in my life. In the past, I felt grief and immense, overwhelming sadness, but this time was different. It was like I was a cold stone, a prelude to the cold darkness of no longer existing.

No, this is not true; I am not supposed to be here. Stoned and lost.

I could feel nothing. Unable to function, I just heard my husband crying. I could only say in response, “I can’t die. I have two little children!”

My thoughts in those stoned moments went to our beautiful babies, Jacob and Leonardo. At the time, they were only three and two, those beautiful, gorgeous potatoes that we finally had after years of struggling. They were finally ours, and I was so happy—finally, I was a mum after years of tribulation.

The pain of possibly not seeing them grow up and leaving them without a mother hit me again even harder than before. I wanted to support them to reach their highest potential.

There and then, my calvary started towards a tortuous and painful finishing line, which I had no clue if it was taking me to another chapter of my life or my very final resting place.

Exactly ten years later, it is not a coincidence that I feel called to talk openly about the effect such an experience had on my life and how this painful journey has paradoxically helped me to develop my potential. Until now, I have buried it somewhere in the corner of my consciousness, not denying it but certainly not giving it the attention, it deserves to reflect on how much it has changed me and helped me to grow as a person and in my professional career as an executive coach.

A cancer diagnosis involves a lot of emotional and then physical pain and uncertainty. I can see now on reflection that after the initial turmoil and once the outcome looked very hopeful, I reconciled with the twisted turn my life was taking: surgery, chemo, radiotherapy, and hopefully recovery.

In the next few pages, I will explain how we can develop our potential by focusing on the things we can control and accepting the things we cannot control. And I will go into detail about a modality called Acceptance and Commitment Therapy (ACT). Through it and with the use of mindfulness, we can truly develop our potential because…

1. We are more attuned to our deep essence.
2. We can uncover our unlimited potential.
3. We focus on what is truly important and surf the waves of life.
4. We develop the courage to change and live to our fullest potential showing up fully for ourselves.

One of my mentors once told me that pain is inevitable, but suffering is optional. This means that sometimes, when life hits us hard after the initial shock, we have to accept the painful events we are facing and the reality of what is. Easy? No! But his point was that whenever we resist our experiences, we increase suffering.

Accepting things as they are does not mean wanting things as they are, but simply being honest and accepting them the way they are. I first learned this concept from my grandma's (beautiful Nonna Wanda) prayers: "God, grant me the serenity to accept the things I cannot change, courage to change the things I can, and wisdom to know the difference."

I truly believe that my Nonna's prayers encompass the true realization of our potential. How so?

I repeatedly studied this concept at school through the teaching of the Stoics first and personal development gurus, such as Steven Covey and other psychologists, after I became a professional coach ten years ago.

The Stoics agreed that within our control are our thoughts, emotions, and interpretations, as well as our reactions and actions. These are the things that we should focus on and work to improve a lifetime of training!

Steve Covey called this the "Circle of Influence."

The Stoics held that there are things that are clearly outside of our control. These include other people's actions, feelings, and opinions of us, the weather, the economy, and random events in life, including major setbacks and traumatic events. Again Steve Covey [1]called it "Circle of concern."

I will delve into how if we focus on the Circle of Influence, we can develop our potential and on the contrary if we focus on the Circle of Concern, where our power and energy get drained, we will just

---

[1] Steve Covey "The Seven Habits of Highly Effective People"

end up in a spiral of helplessness which is exactly the contrary of developing potential.

Now, as the squad of the Circle of Concern includes things that differ from each other, for some of those things, we should not waste our energy worrying about, like other people's actions or reactions or the weather (albeit I often escape the English weather to my native and sunny Italy!) We need to reflect more on some things in the Circle of Concern.

For a traumatic event, acceptance is a difficult but important step in avoiding what we had previously called "suffering." The pain knife is as sharp as a bleeding knife, but we accept it with our thoughts and feelings without fighting them (I know it's so hard, but trust me, it is a profound (spiritual) experience anyone can develop in difficult circumstances.

Acceptance really serves as a deepening of our sense of self with our human limitation: yes, potential is infinite, but we are not, so we need to look at what we can control to develop our potential, and often, we look instead at what we can't. In this way, acceptance focuses our effort toward developing our potential in a realistic way.

Acceptance, in this sense, has been the cornerstone of Acceptance and Commitment Therapy, an action-oriented approach to psychotherapy in which clients stop avoiding, denying, and struggling with their inner emotions and instead accept them as an appropriate response to certain situations that should not prevent them from moving forward with their life.

Another essential element in ACT is cognitive defusion. This means viewing yourself as the "observing self" detached from our "thinking self" .... distancing ourselves from such negative thoughts or beliefs, a process called metacognition.

This phase has been fundamental for me in those dark moments but also in many other crossroads or subsequent difficulties in my life: this is just a belief, and things may go differently, contemplating the possibilities of a different outcome and recognizing our human fragility as a shared common experience.

Just putting a distance between what our mind is flooding our nervous system with and questioning the probability of such an outcome, can clear our mind to focus on more constructive actions, which in ACT are based on our strong values.

Therefore, it is very important to do a value inventory and understand what is important to us so that our values are the guiding light for our actions. In doing so, our potential is not an abstract concept but a concrete action we carry out.

This is important for developing our potential because we can't truly develop it if we are not aligned with what is important to us (our values).

Even in the most difficult circumstances, we will have a clear resonance with what matters to us most, and we want to act according to those values, as there lies and will always be the realization of our potential, purpose, and legacy.

All the above elements of ACT, acceptance, cognitive defusion, values clarification, and commitment to action, lay on the foundation of the last but not least component of ACT, "mindfulness." The last piece needed to reconstruct the jigsaw of our potential.

The modern world's constant distractions obviously take us away from our values and authenticity, though detaching us from our potential. If we are not present with ourselves and the present moment, how can we become the best version of ourselves?? Developing our potential begins from the here and now!

Being present in the present moment allows us to seize the opportunity to notice where we can have an impact and thus develop our potential. If we continue to get distracted by the shining lights of this VUCA (volatility, uncertainty, complexity, and ambiguity) world, we may lose the direction of what is important to us and thus live a life where we follow the "chase," the "rat race," the "fame" rather than our purpose and how to contribute truly, passionately, originally, authentically into this world.

Developing mindfulness, which we have argued is essential for developing potential, is a daily practice that can be exercised, but having a meditation practice can certainly help and speed up the process of aligning with ourselves and thus our potential.

Some ways to increase the power of our mind to be mindful is to be less mind-full: reducing stimulation such as constant use of mobile phones, the internet, or social media (just leave your phone in another room for 30 minutes a day), daydreaming looking outside the window, at the sky or watching people passing by. When I engage in those activities, I am reminded there is a world outside, and my problems are not at the center of the universe, no matter how big they may be.

It is humbling and liberating, as developing our potential is not an egotistic effort but a contribution to society, which brings us closer to our fellow humans.

In our modern society, and this proves even truer for professions such as lawyers, bankers, doctors, and entrepreneurs, we need to avoid filling our agenda with back-to-back activities with no time for a "breather" between them (I believe some people still smoke as an excuse to catch their breath).

Pausing is essential, as it allows our mind to process and organize the information of the previous activity/session. Without it, we jump from one thing to another without savoring any of them. What kind of life can we live if we do not fully engage with every experience? In the end, this reflection resounds profoundly if you have gone through a major life-threatening circumstance. We need to make sense of every moment.

Trying to hustle and be productive every minute of the day is a recipe for your body and brain to burn out.

When we find that rhythm of life sprinkled with mindfulness, we can truly develop our potential because we are more attuned to our deep essence; we can be more productive as we focus on what is truly important and surf the waves of life that sometimes can be challenging.

ACT can promote psychological flexibility to adapt to life's different challenges and circumstances so that the person can learn from any experience, can develop self-compassion as there is a deep acceptance of what is without avoiding discomfort (and thus reducing avoidant behaviors), and develop a deep understanding of "the ebbs and flows of life" as necessary steps to develop us as a full human being [[2].] This allows us to access and realize more of our capabilities and unlimited potential.

A point on avoidant behaviors, which to me, seem to be the opposite of mindfulness: we engage in them in our daily life, sometimes even unconsciously. I am referring, for example, to avoiding situations that can provoke anxiety or discomfort, such as not participating in an event for fear of judgment or fear of failure, a short-term release at the expense of long-term fulfillment (yes, I can be judged, but I can also meet new lovely people and the judgment of naysayers may not affect me that much; also I may accept it as part and parcel of living life). Our potential lives in the unknown in the places we often fear the most. When we move through the fear, we allow ourselves to access higher levels of potential. Mindfulness shows us where we are playing small, which are areas we can expand, unlocking the door to infinite possibilities.

It took me a lot of conscious effort. My journey to become an executive coach from practicing as an international finance lawyer had just begun then.

---

[2] Be a-ware! Mindfulness may not be enough and neither is practicing ACT randomly without the help of a therapist. Mindfulness and ACT may expose people to unresolved trauma, emotions and thoughts that they have been avoiding or denying and, in such circumstances, when you feel very uncomfortable and anxious it is recommended you seek the help a therapist.

I was in the middle of my master's program in executive coaching.[3] and although I was developing a curiosity towards awareness and reflection [.[4]] I was totally upside down physically and emotionally.

Yet, with the help of my family, some friends, and some of my coaching tribe .[5], I could consciously, eventually, accept I had to face such plot twists with compassion, trying not to get caught by the constant negative threatening thoughts, and clarify with my mind that I was allowing cancer to take thirty percent of my life. Meanwhile, doing the best I could to rest, study, start my practice as a coach, being the best mum, and even committing to an adjusted exercise schedule with some jogging, gym and PT sessions.

Setbacks and traumatic experiences, processed thoroughly, can help us live our best lives and truly blossom, thus developing our potential. I learned the most important lesson from my ordeal: time is limited and should be lived in a worthwhile manner. Live less fearfully, take more risks, pursue dreams, and let go of people/relationships/situations that are not meaningful. This is exactly what pursuing our potential is about.

Developing empathy and compassion towards self and others, realizing that we are all on the same boat, the same journey, the

---

[3] I did my now-called Mastered in Business Coaching with the wonderful institute that is Meyler Campbell

[4] John Whitmore, Coaching for Performance, awareness is according with the "godfather of coaching" the cornerstone of coaching together with "responsibility" i.e. the capacity to take charge of our actions

[5] In this instance, I am so grateful to Anne Scolar co-founder and faculty member of Meyler Campbell as she offered to keep my programme on hold yet was respectfully encouraging me to carry on as well as my tutor Andy Barnett and my fellow co-students for their nurturing support and patience during such times.

same “common shared humanity” [.[6]], makes me feel connected to all human beings, albeit we may differ from the outside, and makes me feel less alone, less of a victim of setbacks, and more empathic towards other people.

Going through a traumatic experience can be a great catalyst for growth and developing our potential; most times, it functions as a rest mechanism, smashing all the programs and conditioning from society, childhood, peers, etc., which have kept us caged in life or work to which we did not belong to.

Reframing setbacks to develop our potential and find our true authentic selves, live with purpose, and how we need to contribute to this world is not the only gateway to self-actualization.

Thank Goodness life is not just made of setbacks and trauma. Although we can transform those negative events into meaningful experiences, there are plenty of opportunities to work on our potential on a day-to-day basis, in those ordinary days that can feel “samey” or even “boring.”

If you reflect, though, those are precious times not to be wasted and again lived intentionally to realize ourselves. Yet, I am circling back now to what we have been talking about: the more you have experienced trauma, the more you understand you can’t waste a moment. Your life is not waiting; grab it and go for it every single day!

---

[6] According to Dr. Kristin Neff, common humanity is one of the components of self-compassion together with mindfulness, and self-kindness as read in “Self-Compassion”

I have been coaching for over ten years now after I left my career in international finance law. It was not a simple choice as I enjoyed working as a senior lawyer in investment banking, earning good money, and doing a job that was intellectually stimulating, with brilliant people to work with.

It took me a long time to take the leap of faith, against family and friends' opinions.

In some ways, I was living at my best as a lawyer, and I realized certain aspects of my potential, but something was missing. We often confuse potential with success under societal expectation, but genuine success is something fulfilling to us, not a box-ticking exercise (status, money, interesting work, exposure, career advancement, peer recognition).

I am not saying that these things are not important, but they are a byproduct of knowing we are doing exactly what we are meant to and that we truly love it. Because of this, recognition, money, and success will follow, but they are not the primary focus.

Not relying anymore on what I used to be, on my well-earned career, on my financial stability, and all the habits that come with it have allowed me to go deep inside me and start understanding my desires, the things that were important to me, my values, what I wanted from life on a wider perspective.

My decision was difficult; leaving my profession as a lawyer left me completely bare, without identity/status, and it happened whilst I was just having kids, another milestone in a woman's life where you lose the old you and start again as a new human entity, a mother, so I felt truly raw and bare. Being a mother brings out aspects of you that you did not even know you had. In a way, it creates a new you, and thus, some of the “hidden” potential suddenly seems clear, especially in wanting to leave a legacy for my children but also for future generations.

As a coach, I contribute to other people's potential and growth. If I act in a way that communicates love, respect for self and others, collaboration, and contribution to a better society, then I know I have realized my potential.

I also reflected on what was coming naturally to me, my “strengths,” the things I could easily do without a massive energy drain and would translate into a positive outcome.

It is what Martin Seligman, in positive psychology, calls “meaning”; using your signature strengths to get abundant gratification (through activities we enjoy doing) in the main realms of your life to serve something much larger than you are.

Having a purpose in life helps people focus on what is essential in the face of significant adversity. So, in a way, adversity helps you find meaning, and the meaning helps you realize your potential.

From my experience, all life challenges that question your status quo, identity, and comfort zone are incredible opportunities to reflect and go deeper into knowing yourself. Only from there can you develop your potential, from an authentic connection with yourself, from your genuine desires and passion to reach your goals stemming from this fertile terrain.

In the words of Jimmy Carr, the famous English comic, “It is not the destination nor the journey; it is who we become in that journey.”

"Believe in yourself and all that you are. Know that there is something inside you that is greater than any obstacle."

~ Christian D. Larson

CHAPTER TWELVE

Developing Your Spiritual Mastery

By Grandmother Mulara

Introduction

Another chair is thrown across the room, aimed at an Elder who dared to speak against the supposed community leader's plan. The leader's brothers stood at the doors to the women's toilets to intimidate and physically threaten the Elder women in attendance—thugs. This is what lateral violence looks like. The dynasty of one family hurling abuse and exerting physical means to keep their positions of power, to keep money that flows from government sources and mining royalties within their family.

This was an Australian Aboriginal representative board directors' meeting in the twenty-first century. This was black colonization, black over black.

Ancestral spirit grandmothers came to me in early 2000, wanting to work with me to clean up black colonization. I refused. That would be a death sentence. At the time, I had been undergoing training with senior lore women throughout Aboriginal Australia for thirty years. Ten years passed before I agreed, after I had an epiphany that once we leave our body, our skin suit, we cannot take anything or anyone with us. All that we are is a divine spirit.

Facing initial challenges was the first step towards unlocking my hidden potential. It deepened as the challenges amplified and turned into savage personal attacks.

This is my story of how I unlocked my hidden potential. It begins with a Dreamtime story given to me to fulfil my sacred mission—a story about greed, vanity, and misuse of power and its consequences on an Aboriginal community that I am part of. In exposing corruption, I became a target of hatred and evil and was forced to face a deep well of putrid black poison that unleashed black magic with the desire to kill. The unlocking of my hidden potential to save my life was forged in the fire of spiritual alchemy where I learned about magic and supernatural powers.

My sacred mission would take me on a deeply personal and spiritual journey over the next twelve years, with sickening defamation targeted at me and published throughout the world. It would traverse all levels of corporate law and customary lore, to bankruptcy orchestrated by the supposed community leader, and it would lead me to study a law degree to protect myself.

Sacred Mission

Ancestral spirit grandmothers told me:

> *Your Dreamtime assignment is to quench the thirst of the green lizard.*

Once upon a time, there was a beautiful little green lizard. Everywhere he went, people would comment on how beautiful he was. The little green lizard would shrug and continue to go about his business in innocence, until one day he saw a reflection of himself in a billabong (water hole). "I truly am beautiful," he thought, and he went about the community now taking anything he wanted.
The green lizard began to grow bigger and bigger as he ate up everything in sight, until one day the Lore Keepers decided they had to stop him. He had become too big.
"We must catch the green lizard before he eats everything. If we don't stop him, the land will perish and so will we."
They hatched a plan and caught the green lizard, burying him deep underground. They marked out the area with thirteen cornerstones and proclaimed a warning: "Do not dig him up; should he ever be dug up, the land and the people will perish."
For thousands of years, this Dreamtime story was passed down through the generations in oral tradition.

My Australian Aboriginal ancestors traded in ochre and rocks, including highly prized yellow rocks, now known as uranium. Despite rigorous protests by our Elders, the uranium mining of one of our sacred sites went ahead under the approval of the supposed community leader who was handsomely paid for this permission. I later discovered this supposed community leader was the green lizard.

Against the warning of the Dreamtime story, he was dug up, and the land was perishing, along with the people. Their health deteriorated and the lure of the royalties poisoned their minds. It was not safe for them to stand against the green lizard, for he would use his power against them, and he did. It was a ruthless dictatorship. People were deeply unhappy. They knew something was wrong, so they asked me to help them.

Whistleblower

I asked the grandmothers if they could find someone more qualified. They replied:

> *"We don't call the qualified, we qualify the called . . .*
> *We are calling you, so pick up the phone."*

Some of the Elders and directors contacted me in early 2013 to help them. They gave me the paperwork they had but couldn't read or comprehend themselves because English is not their language. I soon realized the green lizard and his family had set up a company to receive lucrative royalties from other mining industries on our lands. The Elders knew nothing about this company. After I told them, they held a public meeting to let the community know what was happening. The green lizard's family held positions of power in the company and on other director boards.

Five Elders were prepared to put their names on a letter I wrote on their behalf to an office of corporate regulation, seeking to have the company investigated, amongst other concerns. Unfortunately, this letter was in the hands of the green lizard within days. A public servant in the office had improperly passed it on. Corruption was widespread in Aboriginal Australia, including some working in government. Hence, as a whistleblower, I became a target of their vengeance, for the letter to the corporate regulator and the public meeting. I soon learned that repercussions are the price to pay if one crosses the black mafia, as I called them.

Defamation

Initially, I did not know the supposed community leader was the green lizard the grandmothers told me about. When I learned he was one and the same, I changed the reference to "green splat"—an inanimate object—because I decided we like lizards in our country and their character should not be tarnished.

Defamation action over the letter began in 2013 and dragged out for more than eighteen months. It was designed to make an income for the lawyers and drain my resources. Eventually, I had no more money to keep my lawyer or to run a predicted three-week trial, so I dropped my defense to stop it. At the time, I did not know how to tap into my hidden potential.

We settled with a deed whereupon each party was not to disparage the other. It didn't stop them. The green splat with his personal assistant created thirteen different Facebook accounts to continue to defame me. It was sickening, the things they published about me to other Aboriginal communities throughout Australia and the world.

Retaliation for exposing their corruption of millions of dollars activated the green splat's lust for revenge. Aboriginal Australia calls it "payback," good or bad. With the aid of white fella lawyers, the green splat successfully bankrupted me in late 2016. They took everything I had, including my father's inheritance and my car.

It wasn't until six years later when I learned the representative board did not have the legal power to litigate in the first place, or the legal power to bankrupt its own people. I also learned my tribal people did not know he had done that in their name.

Meanwhile, the green splat continued to circulate propaganda about me and the defamation continued. I was powerless to stop him. However, I decided to study a law degree to improve my chances and build my potential.

Our people are all shades of color. My uncle used to say we are like a bag of jellybeans. Original skin color is much lighter in the southern regions of Australia and progressively darkens as we rise in latitude towards the equator. Consequently, those with very dark skin live in the northern areas of Australia. So we are a people with a kaleidoscope of color. Some say we are not white enough and others say we are not black enough. We have a lot of racism in Australia and in our tribes as well. I have been accused of not being Aboriginal because of the pigment of my skin. Some of my uncles told me how they've been on one level regarded as white and on another level not regarded as white, because they aren't.

As a light-skinned woman, I have been able to hide my Aboriginality in white culture. The green splat used the color of my skin to deny I was Aboriginal and a descendant of the tribe. He worked in media so his reach was widespread. The mud thrown at me distracted other tribes as intended and I became famous for being a "fraud." Those who supported me were punished by having their royalties withheld for years or abused in public at meetings and funerals. I was abused at my uncle's funeral in 2023. It was terrible, toxic behavior that no member of the community could be proud of.

My nose is broad and flat. My Aboriginal sisters knew I was one of them. They would often say to me, "Oh, we know you are one of us. Not only are you short, plump, and shiny like we are, you've got our nose."

In time, I launched defamation action against them—firstly the green splat in the magistrate court in 2015, then his family and the representative board for defamation and breach of contract (the deed) in the district court in 2016. Unfortunately, because they had bankrupted me in the federal court, I could not sue for breach of contract and was ordered to pay a sum of $75,000 as a security for costs should I lose the defamation action. Whichever way I looked at it, I was not in a position to fund my pursuit of justice.

The Emotional Toll

It's a horrible feeling to have untrue stories circulated about you and behind your back.

The sense of injustice I felt was deeply traumatic without a way to counter the narrative. The attacks were personal and stressful. I was cyber-hunted like an animal, not only by the black fella brigade but by the white fella "do-gooders" who believed it, although they had never met me. The betrayal of friends who did know me but who chose to believe the narrative was beyond my comprehension. Whatever happened to having a moral compass? Perhaps it was fear of being targeted themselves, of being tarnished with the label "racist" if they didn't comply. The scenario had all the hallmarks of schoolyard bullying and peer group pressure to conform. It was a systemic suppression of truth to maintain a false narrative that privileged a few.

I learned that those for whom I had stood up couldn't stand up for themselves and instead stabbed me in the back. To stand on my principles and not get entangled at their level took courage, inner strength, and willpower. I dug deep within myself to make it through and slowly but surely, I built a level of resilience. I learned that fighting on other people's terms did not work. I decided instead to keep up my daily spiritual prayers and let my work speak for me.

Over the years, my reputation as the person I truly am has outgrown the defamation but not without some emotional scars and suffering glandular fever for two of those years. Unlocking my hidden potential required my body to be healthy and to have a network of people who loved me and believed in me.

Senior Lore Woman

Before white colonization, every original tribe had a senior lore woman and a senior lore man who brought their tribal people through initiation and lore. It was different for me. My maternal grandmother gave my mother to a family in Broken Hill to raise because children with one white parent and one black parent were stolen from their families and raised in institutions. We did not know who our tribe was until my spirit was welcomed back in 2012 and 2013, with three McKenzie Elders recognizing and acknowledging me as one of their own. Nevertheless, senior lore women all over the continent taught me as they ushered me from one tribe to another.

Upon reflection, the senior lore women could see something in me that they nurtured. I was put through levels of initiation, given challenges to overcome, and entrusted with secrets to hold. For over fifty years, I sat at the feet of these esteemed spiritual lore Elders, given the grandmother teachings and the black headband to wear, because I held the grandmother lore. I was also given the Original Women's Lore Staff that had been in my primary lore teacher's lineage for generations, a significant cultural lore practice in my community. In time, my duty will be to pass on the teachings and the lore to the next generation.

With great spiritual power comes great responsibility. The challenges I faced strengthened my knowledge and essential qualities, allowing my potential to become actual abilities. It wasn't always difficult, but this journey did change my life. I worked with the grandmothers. I learned a lot, cried a lot, sang a lot, danced a lot. I was not ever going to be the same after my epiphany and commitment to service and lore walking the right way.

Spiritual Attacks

A spear traveled through the astral field, heading towards me. I saw it in time to turn it around. On another occasion, it was a poisonous snake. One time, a Kadatchi man (lore enforcer) appeared on my doorstep, but I forbade him to enter and commanded him to return to his home. He could not cross the threshold because he did not have permission. I could have succumbed to these black occult spells and curses sent by witch doctors, and then my death would have been attributed to an unexplained accident. These experiences occurred between 2015 and 2018.

On another occasion in 2020, as I worked at my computer, I felt a knife pierce my back. The pain it caused was excruciating, and although I became instantly alert to "someone" inserting a sharp object into my back, there was nobody there. In a conference with a medicine woman, I discovered that inserting a centipede was a particular witch doctor's method of harming people in tropical areas. The tentacles of the black mafia stretched to where I lived in Queensland, and it took a couple of spiritually advanced people to assist me in removing them. The local tribe of Magnetic Island attended to teach the next generation how to remove such a curse even though it existed in another dimension. It was they who instructed my friends on how to remove the centipede.

I was able to spiritually deflect the poison, curses, and efforts to kill me for two main reasons. The first was that I was protected by the lore I carried, for the grandmother lore Is the lore, although this was to mature later in my life. Secondly, I had spent years working on healing myself and developing a spiritual healing practice that strengthened my core. I had to believe in spiritual law, especially the Law of Faith—that I had unseen assistance to get me through this nightmare.

It was my daily spiritual practice that unlocked my potential to withstand black magic aimed to kill me. If I hadn't done the spiritual work, I would be dead.

My life was like a movie, only it was real life.

Defamation Continued

The black mafia struck again.

They did not let up defaming me whenever they could, but it had been sporadic during my bankruptcy period. Now, in 2019, they were under siege because the representative board went into special administration. At long last, the Elders stood up to them and demanded answers. The company was investigated, and fourteen credit cards were found to be directly linked to the account. The dynastic family treated it as if it were their family trust. Where was the $60M+ the uranium mine had paid in royalties? These monies were administered by a master trust over which the green splat had sixty percent control. Legal action through the Supreme Court was launched and, at the time of writing, was in an appeal period after the court had agreed to the appointment of an inspector.

I was blamed for the special administration, even though I was simply minding my own business; however, the time had come to unlock my hidden potential.

The green splat, along with three of his family members, published more defamatory allegations about me in 2019 and 2020. I had had enough and decided to scoop them up again and launch legal proceedings. At first, I used a lawyer, but once again they employed delay tactics such that my resources were depleted. Although I was still studying law at the time of the trial, I was in a far better place to run the trial myself. I strategically sued them as a minor civil claim so they could not impose a security-for-costs order again. Legal representation had to be by consent, which I withdrew. Nevertheless, leaving questions about the judiciary's neutrality to one side, they won.

In 2024, I appealed in the district court on the grounds of a miscarriage of justice and finally had my day in court. The confidence I gained through my law studies helped me to unlock my hidden potential. After twelve years, they had to hear what I had to say without interruption. I proved there was no evidence to support the judgment and that the hearing was prejudicially unfair.

Final Act

Their ultimate act to kill me was to lace the 2023 magistrate's judgment with a vine of wicked spells that exploded when opened. It sent a grenade to my heart. My health declined rapidly, and my heartbeat became erratic. Within two weeks of opening that judgment, I was close to death. I needed help. Thankfully, I have spiritually advanced people in my life who recognized I was in trouble and regulated my heartbeat to theirs until I was strong enough to manage independently. You could say I was given an etheric pacemaker.

A friend and I performed a ceremony in a forest of vines and worked with the ancestors to magically remove the vine from the judgment. In my spiritual peripheral vision, I could see it slowly unwind and retreat. However, there remained a lock of some kind—a spell that would still cause harm if I tried to open it again. Such was the power of black magic. It was sorcery. The green splat paid a witch doctor in a different Aboriginal community to kill me.

I summoned all of my guides and a couple of special friends with magical abilities to track the witch doctor through the astral plane. We found him, enjoying his power and proceeds from crime. He broke our tribal lore, giving me the power to instigate tribal punishment. When he refused to take back the spells and curses, I gave him an ultimatum: either he took everything back, including from women's sacred sites that he had infiltrated (to clean that up was also a responsibility I had as a senior lore woman) or he would bury his grandchildren and have no descendants. That was the lore, and that broke the spell he was under. He fell to his knees, sobbing, "What have I done?" and finally, I was freed.

This series of events not only saved my life but also unlocked my hidden potential as a senior lore woman. I did not know I held that power until I was called upon to use it. The same could be said for other times when danger lurked, such as being circled by a shark in the Maldives when I was board sailing or having a grizzly bear come into my solo camp in Alaska. No point in panicking or being in fear, as that would paralyze me. I only had myself to get out of the situation, to think clearly, and to act with intelligence.

I don't encourage readers to embark on dangerous adventures to overcome fear. However, know that any difficult situation you might find yourself in could present an opportunity to unlock the power and potential already held inside of you.

New Dreaming

There were two sacred missions.

A New Dreaming is coming,
A time when black and white will walk together
Under our sacred traditional lore
That is returned in a new way
When everyone takes responsibility for themselves.
You have to get these teachings out there, girl,
Or people will not know how to look after themselves.

I heard these instructions ringing out from every senior lore woman I ever studied with and some senior lore men—the prophecy of the New Dreaming.

Throughout Terra Australis, the tribal people knew a new day would dawn, a new era when people of all skins would come together. The native peoples of America call it the time of the Rainbow Tribe—a similar prophecy—when the people of the four directions, the four winds, black, white, red, and yellow, come together as one hoop, one circle.

The two missions join because we can't have a New Dreaming until people are ready to take responsibility for themselves. That's part of the new way: walking together, taking responsibility for every footprint we make, our impact on the environment, and our impact on each other. How to heal our relations, how to heal our land, how to connect to spirit, how to heal within—these are the four directions of the sacred circle.

The journey into the New Dreaming begins with sitting at the sacred fire with Elders, the wisdom keepers of ancient lore and knowledge. It's not just sitting; it is learning in action. Holding grandmother lore became my journey on the path to Eldership, where I became the Grandmother.

The spirit grandmothers told me, "You are one of us," that I had chosen to come into this embodiment as a representative of them on the surface of the Earth. I continue to work with my lore Elder, who resides in the Dreaming and with the spirit grandmothers' guidance. It was they who unlocked my potential to complete my sacred missions, to quench the thirst of the green lizard, and to fulfill the greatest role I would play in the unfoldment of the New Dreaming.

As the New Dreaming opens, I am now the Chief Justice of Nmdaka Dalai Australis, our custodial tribal court and sovereign governance. Let us see what the future brings.

"Unlock the doors of possibility by believing in your ability to achieve greatness."

~Marie Forleo

CHAPTER THIRTEEN

From Little Acorns to Mighty Oaks

By John R Spender

"Mighty oaks from little acorns grow."
*~ **Ancient proverb***

Take a stroll in a park or forest. What do you see? Colorful flowers, fruit-bearing shrubs, and tall trees provide shade and shelter to animals and plants. But we seldom stop to think that all this life, all this beauty, this miracle of nature comes from small and humble seeds. Look at what Einstein has achieved for science and humanity; he too was once a little toddler, and not a particularly "brilliant" one it appears. Hidden potential is everywhere, in everything. We live in a world of infinite possibilities. For example, massive trees grow from little seeds, so do geniuses grow from children.

The thing is, we know quite well what trees need to achieve their potential, water, fertile soil, the right climate, but oddly enough, we know very little about how people can do it! Many teachers and gurus have their ways of finding it, but how do you find yours? Everybody has great potential born within them, every newborn child, and every school pupil. It stays with us, even when we are adults, but we don't always know how to express it. So, where can we start?

We can start with ourselves, and in fact, I will start with myself, but follow me as a friend on this journey and relate my story to your experiences. If there is one stable factor that has helped me in my life is not giving up on expanding the potential of who I am.

My parents divorced before I was six, and I didn't come from a financially privileged background. When Dad came home one day, he found only a bowl, plate, knife, fork, and spoon remaining in the house. He was a chief petty officer in the Navy, taking his insecurities out on his young family. It wasn't a safe place for my mother to raise her children. We moved to Manly on the northern beaches of Sydney for six weeks before heading north to my grandparent's cattle station Boonangi, which is the aboriginal name for "place of wild cattle."

Spending a year living with our grandparents with my mum and two siblings created a foundation that instilled the knowing that whatever happened, I could land on my feet and keep going. It was a wholesome experience getting up early in the morning to milk the dairy cow, collecting the chicken eggs, picking the lemons and oranges from the citrus trees for freshly squeezed juice. Walking three kilometres along a dirt road to the school bus stop every morning and after school doing chores around the property taught me the value of fair exchange. The experience was essential to strengthening my resilience, which to me is one of the foundational elements for one to reach their full potential.

Unbeknownst to my family, I had developed learning difficulties because of the trauma I had experienced as a child in a few isolated incidents. I became the class clown and disrupted the lessons anytime it was my turn to read or write. You see, my learning challenges embarrassed me and I had severe dyslexia that wasn't diagnosed until I was in the 8th grade.

Essentially, I was illiterate until I was nine. In 3rd grade, we had a teacher that let us do what we wanted creating an environment of class clowns. The call was strong to reach for my potential, heeding the urge to write and I wrote my first story titled *Sausage Men from Saturn.* It was a mess, and I don't think I spelled a single word correctly. I knew what I was trying to say and what each word meant. I was so proud of my story and felt inspired to show my 2nd grade, teacher Miss Day. She was a benevolent being, always encouraging me despite my often-disruptive nature.

I remember walking across the schoolyard on that sunny day into her class with my little school notebook; you know, the ones with the light blue lines in them. I knocked on her green door, unaware that this moment would be the catalyst to release my dormant potential into a new elevated paradigm. Miss Day stood at the chalkboard, her back slightly turned to students engrossed in taking notes. The door was half open, and she gracefully turned, instantly recognizing me with a smile. Miss Day welcomed me warmly and gestured for me to wait by her desk. As I walked past the desks of my juniors, noticing the handwriting of one particular boy and it was neat, which was the opposite of mine. Feeling embarrassed, I waited next to her desk as Miss Day finished the paragraph she was writing and giving instructions to the class before coming over to me with a sense of delight.

I left her room with words of encouragement and a scratch-and-sniff sticker with an extra spring in my step. In her kind-hearted manner, Miss Day also informed me she would meet with my mom to discuss my story-writing potential.

I wonder: Had they left me alone back then, would I be where I am now? No. Also, would I be who I am now? Certainly not. Fortunately, I listened to my intuition and sought the support of my tenderhearted second-grade teacher. My mother met with Miss Day and compassionately told me about the meeting and how behind I was with my ability. My mom suggested I repeat the third-grade, but Miss Day thought that wouldn't be good for my self-esteem. She had a friend who was a special needs tutor for English. So for almost two years, my tutor Mrs. Brooks taught me the basics of English. My confidence grew and I could read in class.

My teachers helped the young oak withstand the adversity of early life. They showed me which way to grow, which branches to stretch out. Growing is a bit like this; on warm days, we share in the joy and happiness with those around us, and on chilly nights we see who is open to find the light in the stars, and the silver rays of the moon. Then, the sun comes back and there is transformation; expanding our potential creates deep roots, increasing the tree's ability to weather future storms. The oak branches learn to bend rather than break when under pressure.

Unlike many other kids, I soon discovered I had more potential to tap into. In the 5th grade, my mom and granny bought me a rabbit for my birthday. Although initially disappointed to open the box with holes in the top because I was expecting a puppy. BamBam, my albino white rabbit, sure did grow on me. I fell in love with that rabbit. He had the whole back yard to himself and loved the leftover fruits and veggies I got from the local fruit shop. I used to get his favourite food—pears—and hold them in the air, so he had to get up on his back legs and reach up for it.

One of our assignments in class was to write a story about a personal experience. I wrote about BamBam's habit of peeing on people that he didn't know, especially males. He thumped his back legs on the ground, darting around his target before leaping and spraying them. It was so funny even his victims would laugh.

My teacher, Mr. McMahon, loved my story so much that he chose me to represent the class at the story reading contest for all 6th graders. Although I was a lot more confident in my reading ability, reading books for enjoyment. I was still nervous about reading my story to the entire 6th grade and the teachers. I learned early that my potential would not grow in my comfort zone. Preparation was going to be instrumental to reading seamlessly in front of my peers. My mom listened to me as I practised reading my story to her every night for a week before the contest.

On the day I was prepared and less nervous than the other readers, filling me with confidence. With no public speaking experience at all I walked to the front of the assembly hall shaking hands with the contest facilitator. Taking a moment to pause before reading my story with only a couple of stumbles. When I shared how BamBam would wee on my friends, I received plenty of laughs. I finished with a thunderous applause and a few pats on the back from my classmates when I sat down, elevating my sense of potential.

My win in the grade storytelling contest slightly embarrassed me when they announced it. I couldn't believe it. Only three years earlier, I couldn't read a sentence without struggling. I have found over the years that this has been a pattern of mine for discovering a gap in my potential and then learning to grow into the next version of myself. That's the beautiful thing about potential there is no ceiling to how far you can go in pursuing anything in life.

So, let me ask you, is there a void in your life in some area where you are feeling unfulfilled? Maybe you feel stagnant in your career? From my experience, the yearning for more expansion comes first and if it becomes enough of an issue where you are constantly thinking and talking about it, a solution will find you. The hard part is the leap of faith into the unknown. Hence why most people are afraid of their hidden potential and would rather stay the same. At least that way you know what to expect.

Although there isn't as much life force energy in always doing the same old. Yes, it's scary to take ourselves outside our comfort zone. It can also be exhilarating to take a chance on ourselves. What I've found is that everything is an opportunity to transform and grow into a better version of ourselves. It's often hard to realize our potential is increasing when we are going through the challenge or adversity. If we lived a life based on only our senses, you might fool yourself into thinking junk food was good for you. Therefore, it's helpful to have a vision for your life. Without a vision it's easy to become complacent and to allow your environment or the past to consume your thoughts. As an 11- or 12-year-old, I was happy-go-lucky and mostly went with the flow of life. There was always pure potentiality waiting for me.

I played soccer on the weekends for the Kanwal Rovers and the club needed to raise funds for new equipment. The executive community running the club created a raffle, with the first prize being a BBQ set with tables and chairs. This is where it became interesting to me. Whoever sold the most raffle tickets would win a brand new red ten-speed racing bike. The last time I had a new bike I was five. My stepdad was the bulldozer driver at the local rubbish tip and was nifty at putting together bikes. There was nothing wrong with my second-hand bike, but at that age, a ten-speed racing bike was a whole another level of awesome. The potential of it all was exciting and a little daunting. I enlisted a friend of mine to help sell the raffle tickets door to door. I said we could have part ownership swapping each week. However, he didn't have the same drive and dropped out after the first two weeks.

I remained consistent and asked almost everyone that I saw to buy a ticket. I had sold nine books of tickets with a month remaining before the winner was announced. That was ninety tickets sold at a $1 each back in 1987. One of the older high school kids, Matthew Cloney, had sold eleven books of tickets. He was twenty tickets ahead of me. I went to stay the weekend at my uncle's place to mind my cousins. At the time my uncle was a wealthy property developer and owned racehorses. He loved gambling and the weekend was his time to pick the winners. I mustered up the courage to ask him. He was loud and often obnoxious, with a charismatic charm, all of which made me nervous around him.

I knew that timing was everything and he sounded so happy on the phone with the BBQ outside. I walked over and waited for him to finish his call. As soon as he finished, he greeted me with a smile and I asked him in a nervous tone if he would buy some raffle tickets and support my soccer team. He was all in and handed me three twenty-dollar notes and I gave him the six books of tickets explaining the prizes he just gave me this mischievous smile and answered his brick of a mobile phone. It took me a while to process what had just occurred. With focus, determination, and a bit of luck, I won the red ten-speed racing bike.

On the day they declared the winner, I still wasn't sure if I had won. The last time I saw Mrs. Jeffries, the club secretary, she explained it was very close between me, Matthew Cloney and her son Brett Jeffries. So, armed with a set of tickets the week before the announcement, I went door to door to maximise the potential of winning. Sure enough, I had beaten Matthew by fifty tickets. I was over the moon. That bike was the highlight of my young life. It was a fast bike, eating up hills with ease, filling me with confidence. My increase in potential was palpable on the soccer pitch scoring more goals, I had an increase in invites to hang with mates, my grades kept improving and I even made the school cricket team for the first time. I became popular and I enjoyed the attention, especially from the girls. I rode that bike to my first kiss with a girl from another school.

That's potential right there. From no-where and no-thing I could fulfil my potential to reach the goal of winning that red ten-speed racing bike significantly changing my life. That's the power of an unyielding vision on the quantum field of pure potentiality. That early experience with the unified field of infinite potential planted a seed that anything is possible. Are you able to trace back moments in your life where you reached out and touched your highest potential? If you can, I encourage you to journal about the experience, and I think you'll be surprised to see a pattern start to emerge, highlighting your divine blueprint of reaching your highest potential. Once you have that, it's a matter of duplicating that pattern much the same as you would for your favorite recipe.

Affirmations are another great way to expand your potential and believe in infinite possibilities. I found out the power of "will," as a verb… "I want" means "I need." In fact, "I am in want of" means "I lack." On the other hand, "I will" means "I wish into being," or, if you feel confident, "I call into being." I consistently start my days with, "I will show up fully for my clients," or "I will sort out that issue with my sibling." Did it work? Yes, of course! It gave me some reminders of things to do next. It sparked up synapses towards solutions and it rewired my brain to positive paths. I am statements are also powerful. e.g., "I'm abundantly provided for as I follow my path."

Our learning never stops and it's super helpful to have an attitude of a lifelong learner. I'm not sure why some people think learning stops at school, maybe because we stop growing physically. We also think that we stop growing culturally, emotionally, spiritually, and ethically. Maybe we should take a leaf out of trees and plants (pun intended). They never stop growing, and if your potential is an acorn, why stop spreading your branches?

Lifelong education is so accessible, and sometimes even free, or very affordable indeed. There are online courses on every subject, from philosophy to birdwatching; you can work at your own pace and from home; there are some that are mainly or only video-based, others that have written texts.

Then again, there is still the old library you can go to. "Look around you," the opportunities for lifelong learning are virtually infinite.

You know one thing trees are really good at? Adapting! They need to find the space to grow, both roots and branches. They bend to the wind; they stretch underground to find water and nutrients. Maybe this is why they can grow forever.

When you think about your life, your education, your career, your relationships, imagine you are a tree. If a path is definitely close to you, lean to the side. If you cannot grow a branch, grow another one higher up…

Many techniques we have seen will develop your adaptability, from mindfulness to meditation, but you need to keep this in mind: life is always changing, and the world is doing it fast. So, always stop to assess if there are routes, paths that will suit you better than the one you are on.

Imagine walking along a country lane, and finding yourself in a place you don't fully enjoy; what would you do? Look for an alternative path, or maybe take a few steps back to the last junction and try the other way.

Life is not that fixed moment in time; it is the flow of our consciousness from the past to the future. The moment is only a series of crossroads, and if you take each alternative path as an opportunity, you will always find a way to fulfill your potential.

In the end, trees fork out branches and roots too; and sometimes, they abandon a branch and give their energy to another.

Now is the time to reflect. Take a break and enjoy a walk in the park or forest. Let nature inspire your growth. When you breathe in the fresh air, think of yourself as an acorn, and visualize growing into an enormous oak tree, or, why not, an entire forest.

“We all have the potential to be extraordinary. We just have to unlock it.”

~ Jay Shetty

AUTHOR BIOGRAPHIES

Catalina Galeano

CHAPTER ONE

Catalina Galeano is a passionate wisdom keeper and transformational leader, born in Zipaquirá, Colombia, and the proud mother of a radiant 13-year-old daughter. Deeply committed to personal and collective evolution. Her life mission is to guide others on profound journeys of self-exploration, personal development, and spiritual expansion.

As a transformational coach and alchemist, Catalina guides individuals to break free from limiting beliefs and conditioned patterns, awakening them to their inner power and divine essence. She believes true transformation begins when we shed the layers that no longer serve us, allowing us to step fully into our authentic selves.

With a diverse background in venture capital, commercial real estate, and mortgage lending, Catalina blends practical expertise with deep spiritual insight to offer solutions that not only transform lives but also elevate people's potential on all levels—mind, body, and soul. Her approach, a powerful fusion of grounded wisdom and visionary guidance, makes her work both transformative and life-changing.

Catalina's personal journey of self-healing and expansion has led her to explore a wide range of mystical and holistic practices, including hypnosis, Reiki, EFT Tapping, family constellations, Vipassana meditation and Toltec wisdom. Her most profound transformation, however, came through the sacred power of plant medicine, a pivotal experience that awakened her natural shamanic gifts and deepened her connection to the divine.

Catalina stands as a beacon for those ready to awaken their highest truths, inviting others to step into their power and live as the divine creators of their own lives.

Contact details:
https://www.soulchingalchemy.com/
soulchingalchemy@gmail.com
Virtual Card - https://blinq.me/JbA4nA4wdXXIE44yjM0Q?bs=db

Rebecca Shannon

CHAPTER TWO

Rebecca is a Mother to three boys, a leadership and empowerment coach with her own private practice, and is known for her trademark 'hot pink' branding.

She lives in North Kent, England, in a gorgeous townhouse on a tidal creek, along with her sons, two cats, and Avocets, Herons, and Egrets as her neighbours.

Rebecca has adopted a uniquely holistic approach to coaching. Her philosophy is underpinned by the belief that if your personal life is out of kilter you'll never be able to show up at work and fulfil your true potential. She helps people with all aspects of their lives, from the intensely private to published corporate goals.

Rebecca loves to sing, write, and travel and is committed to forever learning and creating a life she loves full of purpose and passion.

Mindful, intuitive, and curious, Rebecca creates hot pink ripples in the world that sparkle and shine through her love and light.

Rebecca's website: www.complementcoaching.com
Rebecca's email: rebecca@complementcoaching.com
Rebecca's LinkedIn: https://www.linkedin.com/in/rebecca-shannon

Cari Rickabaugh

CHAPTER THREE

Cari has always been a passionate advocate for service and helping others, starting at age 21 when she dedicated 1 ½ years to a proselytizing mission with the LDS Church. Now with 23 years of experience as a Massage Therapist and thirteen years as a Master Bodyworker. Her work is a natural extension of her desire to help improve the lives of others.

Cari has worked in diverse settings, including clinics, with chiropractors, and with a Major League Soccer team, in addition to building her own practice. Her goal has always been to help people function better, enhancing their quality of life.

More recently, Cari became a Life and Trauma Resolution coach, guiding individuals through personal obstacles and supporting those who have experienced sexual assault and trauma. Through her coaching, she offers more than just healing—she provides the strength and courage to fully embrace life. In the past year and a half, she has created a distinctive approach that combines bodywork, coaching, and energy healing, empowering clients to embrace life fully and achieve holistic healing for both mind and body.

Cari is also a public speaker, and has spent many years working in theatre, both on stage and behind the scenes. She currently resides in Wisconsin, where she enjoys the beauty of Lake Michigan and multiple state parks, often running and cold plunging. Her life journey—spanning unique experiences like talent agent and horse-drawn carriage driver, as well as the trauma she has overcome—reflects her eclectic interests, resilience, dedication to empowering others, and commitment to healing.

Contact: Resiliencemindandbodycoaching@outlook.com
Website: ResilienceMindandBodyCoaching.com

Ben Welch

CHAPTER FOUR

After living restricted and conditioned by the fundamentalist religious beliefs of his upbringing. Ben at 30 took a machete to his childhood conditioning, instead cutting his own path and navigating life in many ways that coincide with this book - seeking out his hidden potential by all means necessary.

With several careers spanning over different industries from building and construction to sales, personal training and transformational coaching. He has developed a personal and professional focus on observing and renovating life beginning with the foundation and having a construction like principle based approach to observing one's self. Being open to the cracks that affect one's emotional, psychological, spiritual and material experiences of life which clearly point to the truth of who we are.

Then newly constructing a life on purpose as the human one is committed to being.

A father of five children at this time of writing between 13 and 21 and husband to beautiful Melissa for 24 years, Ben has carried out this process amongst the joys and challenges of marriage, the loss of a child and child rearing, overcoming grief and depression and instead choosing commitment to a place of living with patience in the discovery of who he is for himself and in turn others.

Ben loves to support others in this process and lives with passion and wonder for the stories of how the world opens up for all humans. When they choose to live actively in the arena of life bringing courage and vulnerability with strength and power to life. He loves to watch their expansion with joy, honor and respect. And see the renovation potential we all are advance from fear and lack into service and success.

Email: ben@benwelch.co
Facebook: @benwelch.co

Corrina Bowcott

CHAPTER FIVE

From a young age, Corrina was free-spirited, with a deep-seated purpose to be different. Her innate ability to see the world through a unique lens paved the way for her future to help others find their own paths to healing and self-discovery. Corrine's journey has been anything but conventional, marked by resilience, transformation, and an unwavering commitment to personal growth.

At 23 years old, Corrina faced the greatest challenge of her life when she was diagnosed with cancer. This life-altering experience served as the catalyst for her path of self-discovery, igniting a deep desire to understand herself and the world around her. However, the shadows of a toxic family dynamic and abusive relationships continued to impact her life, yet she still fought for survival and healing.

Corrina's quest for understanding led her to dive deep into the world of energy work. She became a Reiki Master and obtained multiple certifications in coaching, honing her skills in helping others with their own intuitive wisdom. Driven by her experiences, she also volunteered to counsel others at a local shelter, solidifying her commitment to supporting people.

In addition to her work in healing and coaching, Corrina's entrepreneurial spirit led her to establish three successful pet grooming salons and a thriving restaurant, demonstrating her ability to manifest success in multiple industries. Today, she is on the path to becoming a sought-after Intuitive Coach and author, combining her personal experiences with her extensive training to inspire and guide others toward a life of purpose and fulfillment.

Patrick Richard Garcia

CHAPTER SIX

Patrick Richard Garcia is a two-time international best-selling author, transformative & development strategist, results coach, and owner of Hustle Revival Enterprises. He helps entrepreneurs revive their hustle instincts through result-producing and intensive self-development activities simultaneously.

Patrick is also an inspirational speaker, starting his first on-stage appearance on June 2017 at Speaker Slam: So You Think You Can Speak? Thereon, he started his journey in further developing his craft in storytelling and competing in competitions on and offline. His most recent competition was on September 2023 at Speaker Slam: Perseverance, sharing his powerful story regarding his learning disability and the adversity involved to be presently where he is today.

Driven by his life experiences, he takes pride in providing the best results possible.

Patrick currently resides in Toronto, ON, Canada and is married to his wife, Grace.

Laura Jean Denman

CHAPTER SEVEN

Laura was born and raised in Southampton, a town in the south of England, famously known as the sailing port of the Titanic. She is married and has three amazing children, which was always one of her life goals. As a huge lover of animals, she also enjoys caring for her adored pets.

Laura created a small business focused on her passion for well-being, with the aim of connecting with her local community. Her hope was that, after the effects of Covid, people would come together again to improve their health and well-being through yoga, social events, women's circles, and retreats both in the UK and abroad.

Yoga naturally led to Laura's interest in personal development and life coaching. After becoming a certified life coach, she worked alongside the crew at Tony Robbins' Unleash the Power Within events. Laura now applies her skills at retreats and women's empowerment circles.

She envisions projects where she helps women explore their personal stories through writing, self-love retreats, circle sharing, and positive affirmations. These projects aim to foster self-discovery and unlock their full potential. Writing this chapter has been a healing process for Laura, which she hopes to share with others.

This chapter is dedicated to Laura's late father, David Channell

Laura is using Coldplay's music as her dedicated songs, believing that her opportunity manifested through this connection.

"Daddy" by Coldplay – Her PAIN song
"Sky Full of Stars" by Coldplay – Her HOPE song

Laura's email: puravidawellbeing@gmail.com
Instagram: @puravidawellbeing
Website: Puravidawellbeingcentre.co.uk

Lynn Hayward

CHAPTER EIGHT

Lynn Hayward: Turning Pain into Purpose through Art and Innovation

Lynn Hayward, a Scottish-born artist, author, and digital innovator, transforms challenges into creativity. Spanning four decades across Scotland, Zimbabwe, and Australia. Her journey blends traditional artistry and cutting-edge digital mediums to inspire growth, resilience, and healing.

A finalist in the 2004 Scottish Women exhibition at Edinburgh's National Portrait Gallery, Lynn has reimagined her creative process after a Complex Regional Pain Syndrome (CRPS) diagnosis in 2020. Turning adversity into opportunity, she uses art and writing as tools to "turn her pain volume down" and empower others.

As a two-time contributor to the *A Journey of Riches* anthology series, her first edition, *Elevate Your Life: Reimagining the Nexus of Art*, earned Amazon #1 bestseller status. Lynn's latest work, *My Cosmic Leap: Illuminating and Outlining the Invisible Nexus Within*, inspires readers to align with their creativity and uncover infinite opportunities.

As the founder of **360° Step Forward Nexus**, Lynn champions CRPS and pain awareness with #CreativeSolutionsThroughAdversity. She develops transformative tools like the Creative Visual Assistant (CVA), mindfulness-based coloring books, as well as non-fiction writing and creative courses to help others turn pain into purpose and unlock their limitless potential.

Join Lynn on her transformative journey, where art becomes therapy, resilience fuels creativity, and every stroke lights the path forward. 2025 promises to amplify her #alignwithauthenticity hashtag.

Connect with Lynn

- **Website** (coming soon): www.360StepForward.com
- **Email**: studioartfulnow@gmail.com
- **Social Media**:
    - Artful Now Studio Instagram
    - Backyard Adventures Instagram
    - Facebook
    - YouTube
    - Twitter

Darlene Doiron

CHAPTER NINE

Darlene was born and raised in New Brunswick, Canada, and has led a diverse and adventurous career path. Her professional journey spans working as an aesthetician, serving passengers on VIA Rail trains, nursing, driving 18-wheelers, and operating some of the largest trucks in the mining industry.

Most recently, she worked as a dispatcher for a mining company—roles that have taken her across Canada and ultimately led her to call Alberta home.

An avid traveler, Darlene has a deep love for exploring the world. However, her greatest passion lies in helping others. Through writing this chapter, she hopes to inspire and make a difference, even if it touches just one person's life.

Darlene is now prioritizing her health, embracing each day, and living life to the fullest.

Ewelina Korus

CHAPTER TEN

Ewelina has spent fourteen transformative years living in a foreign country, fulfilling her dreams and turning them into reality. She is passionate about mindset, interior design, photography, and travel, and is deeply committed to self-development, guided by an unwavering connection to her inner voice. From a young age, Ewelina intuitively applied visualization techniques, setting goals that have successfully come to fruition.

Her journey has been enriched by learning from some of the most influential experts in personal development and mindset mastery. These profound experiences have equipped her with the tools and insights needed to express her true self and help others do the same. Ewelina encourages increasing the energy needed to visualize and manifest a dream life on a higher frequency with quick results.

Understanding the various challenges life can present—from career and finances to relationships and building her own business—Ewelina emphasizes the transformative power of a strong mindset. Her mission is to guide women to harness their own potential and visualize and manifest a life they truly deserve. By 2025/2026, she envisions expanding her impact through retreats that encourage women to live authentically and fully.

To explore more of Ewelina's insights and be inspired by her journey, visit her website:
https://ekpositivemindset.com/

Connect via her Facebook profile:
https://www.facebook.com/EwelinaaaKorus/
https://www.facebook.com/groups/empoweredglobalwomen.

Her chapter, "The Power Within," in the bestselling book *Unlock Your Hidden Potential*, is a testament to her commitment to personal growth and empowerment.

Transformative New You Program for Women to Step into Your Power, Visualize, Manifest, and Transform Your Life Using Your Authentic Feminine Potential.

Link: https://payhip.com/b/5HsYI

For those who bought this book, receive a 10% discount by signing up using the code POTENTIAL10%.

Annelise Pesa

CHAPTER ELEVEN

Annelise is an executive coach and corporate trainer with a specialized focus on lawyers and senior professionals.

With connection to Italy, US, UK, and Australia, she thrives through different cultures and travelling.

Drawing from her extensive background as an international finance lawyer—head of Legal for Morgan Stanley, and senior associate at Clifford Chance and Linklaters—Annelise empowers leaders and teams to maximize their potential and pursue authentic goals by leveraging their unique strengths and desires.

Her expertise includes leadership development, career progression, team coaching, and fostering resilience and well-being in the workplace.

Annelise works always start with the whole person, for true lasting change and growth, before seeing the professional, which is only one aspect of the wider "human system."

She holds a Magna Cum Laude degree in Law from the University of Rome and a Master's in Banking and Finance Law from the University of London. Annelise also has many coaching credentials including a Master in Business Coaching from Meyler Campbell, certifications in NLP, Positive Psychology and Well Being, Trauma-Informed Coaching, Stress Management and Resilience, and Agile Team Coaching. She is a PCC by ICF.

Annelise lives with her family in London.

Please send her an email to annelise@annelisepesa.com and visit annelisepesa.com

Grandmother Mulara

CHAPTER TWELVE

Grandmother Mulara is an Aboriginal Elder and Senior Lore/Law Woman who also holds a Juris Doctor in colonial law. She was taught for over 50 years by generations of Senior Lore Elders throughout Terra Australis and was given responsibility for Grandmother Lore teachings. Grandmother Mulara walks between two cultures and two laws, bringing through the New Dreaming, *Wirritjin*, as prophesied by Elders a long time ago, a time when humanity will walk together under the return of natural law and the traditional lore of the land.

She is a master healer and educator, an executive coach and leadership consultant. Grandmother Mulara has led expeditions in many parts of Australia and overseas; researched values, ethics and leadership at PhD level; having received numerous awards for her work, including an Australian Prime Minister's Award of Merit. Her Aboriginal lineage comes from her grandfather, Archie McKenzie, from the Northern Flinders Ranges, and her grandmother a descendant from Wilcannia/Broken Hill country and Afghani camel drivers.

Grandmother Mulara is highly sought after throughout the world for her spiritual wisdom and life experience. She conducts ceremonies and offers classes in Developing Spiritual Mastery and in Women's Lore. Grandmother Mulara can be contacted through her website, www.grandmotherwisdom.com.

John R Spender

CHAPTER THIRTEEN

John R. Spender is a 38-time International Best-Selling co-author who didn't learn how to read and write at a basic level until he was ten years old. He has since traveled to more than 70 countries and territories and started many businesses, leading him to create the best-selling book series *A Journey of Riches*. He is also an award-winning international speaker and movie maker.

John worked as an international NLP trainer and coached thousands of people from various backgrounds through many challenges. From borderline homeless individuals to wealthy people, he has helped many connect with their truth to create a life on their terms.

His search for answers to living a fulfilling life has taken him to work with Native American Indians in the Hills of San Diego, visit the forests of Madagascar, swim with humpback whales in Tonga, explore the Okavango Delta of Botswana, and climb the Great Wall of China. John has traveled from Chile to Slovakia, Hungary to the Solomon Islands, the mountains of Italy, and the streets of Mexico.

Everywhere his journey has taken him, John has discovered a hunger among people to find a new way to live, with a yearning for freedom of expression. His belief that everyone has a book in them was born.

He is now a writing coach, having worked with over 400 authors from 50 countries for the *A Journey of Riches* series (http://ajourneyofriches.com/). His publishing house, Motion Media International, has published 45 non-fiction titles to date.

John also co-wrote and produced the movie documentary *Adversity,* which will be released in 2025, and stars Jack Canfield, Rev. Michael Bernard Beckwith, Dr. John Demartini, and many more. You can bet there will be a best-selling book to follow!

"Unlocking your potential starts with discovering the strengths you already have within you."

~ Les Brown

AFTERWORD

I hope you enjoyed the heartfelt stories, wisdom, and vulnerability shared. Storytelling is the oldest form of communication, and I hope you feel inspired to take a step toward living a fulfilling life. Feel free to contact any of the authors in this book or the other books in this series.

The proceeds of this book will be used for social giving at Jewel Children's Home in Northeast Bali.

Other books in this series include...

Follow Your Soul's Calling, Book Thirty-Eight
https://www.amazon.com/dp/B0DQJYLBHY

The Power of Self-Discovery, Book Thirty-Seven
https://www.amazon.com/dp/B0D4K35JFP

Elevating Your Life: A Journey of Riches, Book Thirty-Six
https://www.amazon.com/dp/B0CZWRJ94Y

Living the Paradigm of Kindness: A Journey of Riches, Book Thirty-Five
https://www.amazon.com/dp/B0CSXF1FBV

Creating Resilience: A Journey of Riches, Book Thirty-Four
https://www.amazon.com/dp/B0CNVRDY38

Discover Your Purpose: A Journey of Riches, Book Thirty-Three
https://www.amazon.com/dp/B0CFDLWTCB

Live Your Passion: A Journey of Riches, Book Thirty-two
https://www.amazon.com/Live-Your-Passion-Stories-Fulfilling-ebook/dp/B0C5QXMNRQ

Master Your Mindset: A Journey of Riches, Book Thirty-one
https://mybook.to/MasterYourMindset

Transform Your Wounds into Wisdom: A Journey of Riches, Book Thirty
https://www.amazon.com/dp/ B0BKTJ377N

Motivate Your Life: A Journey of Riches, Book Twenty-Nine
https://www.amazon.com/dp/B0BCXMF11P

Awaken to Your Inner Truth: A Journey of Riches, Book Twenty-Eight
https://www.amazon.com/dp/B09YLYMQ4H?geniuslink=true

The Power of Inspiration: A Journey of Riches, Book Twenty-Seven
http://mybook.to/ThePowerofInspiration

Messages from The Heart: A Journey of Riches, Book Twenty-Six
http://mybook.to/MessagesOfHeart

Abundant Living: A Journey of Riches, Book Twenty-Five
https://www.amazon.com/dp/B0963N6B2C

The Way of the Leader: A Journey of Riches, Book Twenty-Four
https://www.amazon.com/dp/1925919285

The Attitude of Gratitude: A Journey of Riches, Book Twenty-Three
https://www.amazon.com/dp/1925919269

Facing Your Fears: *A Journey of Riches,* Book Twenty-Two
https://www.amazon.com/dp/1925919218

Returning to Love: *A Journey of Riches,* Book Twenty-One
https://www.amazon.com/dp/B08C54M2RB

Develop Inner Strength: *A Journey of Riches,* Book Twenty
https://www.amazon.com/dp/1925919153

Building your Dreams: A Journey of Riches, Book Nineteen
https://www.amazon.com/dp/B081KZCN5R

Liberate your Struggles: A Journey of Riches, Book Eighteen
https://www.amazon.com/dp/1925919099

In Search of Happiness: A Journey of Riches, Book Seventeen
https://www.amazon.com/dp/B07R8HMP3K

Tapping into Courage: A Journey of Riches, Book Sixteen
https://www.amazon.com/dp/B07NDCY1KY

The Power Healing: A Journey of Riches, Book Fifteen
https://www.amazon.com/dp/B07LGRJQ2S

The Way of the Entrepreneur: A Journey of Riches, Book Fourteen
https://www.amazon.com/dp/B07KNHYR8V

Discovering Love and Gratitude: A Journey of Riches, Book Thirteen
https://www.amazon.com/dp/B07H23Q6D1

Transformational Change: A Journey of Riches, Book Twelve
https://www.amazon.com/dp/B07FYHMQRS

Finding Inspiration: A Journey of Riches, Book Eleven
https://www.amazon.com/dp/B07F1LS1ZW

Building your Life from Rock Bottom: A Journey of Riches, Book Ten
https://www.amazon.com/dp/B07CZK155Z

Transformation Calling: A Journey of Riches, Book Nine
https://www.amazon.com/dp/B07BWQY9FB

Letting Go and Embracing the New: A Journey of Riches, Book Eight
https://www.amazon.com/dp/B079ZKT2C2

Making Empowering Choices: A Journey of Riches, Book Seven
https://www.amazon.com/Making-Empowering-Choices-Journey-Riches-ebook/dp/B078JXMK5V

The Benefit of Challenge: A Journey of Riches, Book Six
https://www.amazon.com/dp/B0778S2VBD

Personal Changes: A Journey of Riches, Book Five
https://www.amazon.com/dp/B075WCQM4N

Dealing with Changes in Life: A Journey of Riches, Book Four
https://www.amazon.com/dp/B0716RDKK7

Making Changes: A Journey of Riches, Book Three
https://www.amazon.com/dp/B01MYWNI5A

The Gift In Challenge: A Journey of Riches, Book Two
https://www.amazon.com/dp/B01GBEML4G

From Darkness into the Light: A Journey of Riches, Book One
https://www.amazon.com/dp/B018QMPHJW

Thank you to all the authors who have shared aspects of their lives, hoping to inspire others to live a bigger version of themselves.

I want to share a beautiful quote from Jim Rohn: “You can’t complain and feel grateful at the same time.” At any given moment, we can either feel like a victim of life or be connected and grateful for it. I hope this book helps you feel grateful and inspires you to pursue your dreams.

For more information about contributing to the series, visit http://ajourneyofriches.com/. Furthermore, if you enjoyed reading this book, we would appreciate your review on Amazon to help get our message out to even more readers.

www.ingramcontent.com/pod-product-compliance
Lightning Source LLC
Chambersburg PA
CBHW051950090426
42741CB00008B/1341
* 9 7 8 1 9 2 5 9 1 9 8 6 8 *